Here Bob Fyall takes you in ...
clinic, and teaches you to fee ...
current?) of the narratives in 2 ...
often jump out from his obsei vaiiuns, ..., ...,
miss those, the leading questions are lasered in on all the
essential matters that will open up the text. Timid souls
who, either from fear or lethargy have avoided preaching
from 2 Kings, are now 'without excuse.'

Dale Ralph Davis
Respected Author and Old Testament Scholar

Bob Fyall on the text of Scripture is as good to read as to
hear. Recommended.

Dick Lucas
Formerly Rector of St Helen's Bishopsgate, London

This is an excellent book to aid anyone who wants a better
understanding of 2 Kings. Bob Fyall has given us an
imaginative, perceptive and practical tool that flows from
his own preaching and will assist anyone who wants to
preach Christ from 2 Kings. It is highly recommended.

Paul Mallard
Pastor of Widcombe Baptist Church, Bath, UK
Speaker and author of several books

TEACHING
2 KINGS

From text to message

BOB FYALL

SERIES EDITORS: JON GEMMELL & DAVID JACKMAN

PT RESOURCES

CHRISTIAN
FOCUS

Copyright © Proclamation Trust Media 2019

ISBN: 978-1-5271-0157-9

10 9 8 7 6 5 4 3 2 1

Published in 2019

by

Christian Focus Publications Ltd,
Geanies House, Fearn, Ross-shire,
IV20 1TW, Scotland, Great Britain

with

Proclamation Trust Resources,
Willcox House, 140-148 Borough High Street,
London, SE1 1LB, England, Great Britain.
www.proctrust.org.uk

www.christianfocus.com

Cover design by Moose77.com

Printed and bound by
Bell & Bain, Glasgow

Contents

SERIES PREFACE

Like many Bible books containing Old Testament narrative, 1 and 2 Kings are both familiar because of the purple passages they contain but also obscure because of the parts we seldom read and steer away from in our preaching. Some of the stories of 1 and 2 Kings we have grown up with in Sunday school, whereas others are skimmed over as the reigns of despotic idolatrous kings are summarised in a few short verses.

This pick and mix approach to this epic narrative needs to be addressed, and rather than go for selected highlights, these books of 1 and 2 Kings deserve to be handled on their own terms, honouring their unity and doing justice to their overarching themes. This book of Kings has been breathed out by God and therefore is in its entirety profitable for us (2 Tim. 3:16).

This is the second volume that Bob Fyall has written in our Teaching the Bible series on the book of Kings, this one on the book of 2 Kings. This volume like the first is such an aid to anyone preaching, teaching or reading

2 Kings as it informs, excites, enthuses and encourages you to dig deeper into the stories that we are familiar with and also to understand the parts that are too often ignored. Bob's tracing of the line of the Davidic King is so helpful in shaping our understanding of these books.

This volume, like all in the series, are written with the Bible teacher and Bible student in mind. Part One, the introductory section, contains lots of important information to help us get a handle on the book of 2 Kings, covering aspects like structure, place in the Biblical story and also great assistance on how you would go about planning a preaching series. Then Part Two and Part Three work through the book systematically giving insight into the text as well as suggesting sermon outlines, key applications and also Bible study questions. These are not there to take the hard work out of preparation but to be a helping hand as people invest their time, efforts and gifts in preparing to teach the Bible to others.

Teaching 2 Kings brings the number of published volumes in this series to twenty. We are encouraged by how this series is developing and the comments we hear from people involved in regular Bible teaching and preaching ministry. We long for these books to help people to keep working hard at the Word in order that they might proclaim the unsearchable riches of Christ ever more clearly.

Our thanks go to Christian Focus for their continued partnership in this project. Without their faith, expertise and patience none of these books would ever make it on to the bookshelf. Thanks must also go to Geraldine Sparks and Charlotte Bailey in the PT office who took the editorial

scribbles of Jon Gemmell and transferred them skilfully to
the manuscript.

Jon Gemmell & David Jackman
Series Editors
London 2018

Author's Preface

Three outstanding history teachers in my schooldays gave me an abiding love for the subject and showed how the past could live in the hands of gifted and imaginative communicators. This easily transferred to a love of Biblical history and narrative. The books of 1 and 2 Kings have therefore been a part of Scripture I have long enjoyed, and when I started to study the Old Testament seriously I returned to them with renewed interest and with a growing appreciation of their great importance in the big story and their powerful message for today.

Probably like most preachers who tackle these books, I turned first to the Elijah/Elisha stories with their compelling characters and strong narrative drive. However, it soon became apparent that these stories were even more compelling when seen in the overall flow of the books.

Over the years I have preached both longer and shorter series on the books. In my first ministry in Bannockburn, I did a series of moderate length on Elijah and Elisha. In my years in Durham, in the congregation now known as

Christchurch (then Claypath) a number of series were preached and, I trust, a growing understanding of the overall message emerged. A longer series, covering much of both books, was preached in the Tron Church, Glasgow over the period 2008 – 2010.

I have also had the privilege of teaching large sections of the book in other contexts. In 2002 – 2005 I taught a module on 'Preaching OT narrative' in Crammer Hall, St John's College, Durham where I was once on the staff. That module was repeated at the International Christian College, Glasgow in 2007. At Cornhill Scotland, I often use material from Kings, especially when teaching how to preach Biblical narrative.

Plainly I have gained a great deal from those who have commented on the sermons and lectures and I am most grateful for that. I have also learned much from commentators, and mention that in the 'Further Reading' section. As always, I have learned from those I disagree with and am thankful for all whose work has fed into mine.

This *Teaching* book has also given me the opportunity to engage with parts of the books I have passed over lightly in the past. I trust it will encourage others to study Kings as a whole and not simply pick out the purple passages. The length can be daunting but when we consider that the time covered is some five hundred years we see that the author has been ruthlessly selective in including what carries on his theme.

Like the other *Teaching* volumes this is not a commentary, although it engages closely with the text, nor simply a collection of sermons although there are suggested sermons and Bible study questions. Thus it will be most useful if the reader does some detailed exegetical work on the text first. Often there is more than one suggested sermon outline to emphasise that once you really get into what the passage says there are many ways of expressing and applying the message.

It is my prayer that this book will help many to explore the books of Kings and be captured by their riches and preach and teach their God-honouring and Christ-anticipating message.

Bob Fyall
Glasgow 2019

PART ONE:
INTRODUCING KINGS

How to Use this book

This book aims to help the preacher or teacher understand the central aim and purpose of the text, in order to preach or teach it to others. Unlike a commentary, therefore, it does not go into great exegetical detail. Instead it helps us to engage with the themes of Kings, to keep the big picture in mind, and to think about how to present it to our hearers.

'Part One: Introducing Kings' examines the book's themes and structure as well as seeing why it is considered a difficult book to preach. This material is crucial to our understanding of the whole book, which will shape the way we preach each section to our congregations. As a preliminary to the rest of the book, it divides the two Bible books up into manageable units. This preliminary work leaves us with three major sections: 1 Kings 1–11, 1 Kings 12 – 2 Kings 17 and 2 Kings 18–25. These will be covered over two volumes with, for ease of use, 1 Kings being considered in volume 1 and 2 Kings in volume 2.

The remainder of the two volumes contains separate chapters on each preaching unit considered in Part One.

The structure of each chapter is the same: it begins with a brief introduction to the unit followed by a section headed 'Listening to the text.' This section outlines the structure and context of the unit and takes the reader through a section by section analysis of the text. All good biblical preaching begins with careful, detailed listening to the text and this is true for Kings as much as any other book.

Each chapter then continues with a section called 'From text to message.' This suggests a main theme and aim for each preaching unit (including how the unit relates to the overall theme of the book) and then some possible sermon outlines. These suggestions are nothing more than that – suggestions designed to help the preacher think about his own division of the text and the structure of the sermon. We are great believers in every preacher constructing his own outlines, because they need to flow from our personal encounter with God in the text. Downloading other people's sermons or trying to breathe life into someone else's outlines are strategies doomed to failure. They may produce a reasonable talk, but in the long term, they are disastrous to the preacher himself since he needs to live in the Word and the Word to live in him, if he is to speak from the heart of God to the hearts of his congregation. However, these sections provide a few very basic ideas about how an outline on some of these passages might shape up. There are also some helpful bullet points on possible lines of application with particular focus on how lines to Christ may be drawn.

Each chapter concludes with some suggested questions for a group Bible study split into two types: questions to help *understand* the passage and questions to help *apply* the passage. Not all the questions would be needed for a study, but they give some ideas for those who are planning a study series.

The aim of good questions is always to drive the group into the text, to explore and understand its meaning more fully. This keeps the focus on Scripture and reduces speculation and the mere exchange of opinions. Remember the key issues are always, 'What does the text say?' and then 'What does it mean?' Avoid the 'What does it mean to you?' type of question. It is much better to discuss the application more generally and personally after everyone understands the intended meaning, so that the Bible really is in the driving-seat of the study, not the participants' opinions, prejudices or experiences! These studies will be especially useful in those churches where Bible study groups are able to study the book at the same time as it is preached, a practice we warmly commend. This allows small groups to drive home understanding, and especially application, in the week after the sermon has been preached, ensuring it is applied to the daily lives of the congregation.

INTRODUCING 2 KINGS

Getting our bearings in 2 Kings

For many, tackling the books of Kings is like embarking on a rather unfamiliar sea with just a few well known islands, such as some of the stories of Elisha and Elijah. We reach these with relief and see the rest of the voyage as rather tedious and uninspiring. The brief notes on individual kings in passages such as 1 Kings 15 and 16 or 2 Kings 13–15, not to say the long details of temple building in 1 Kings 6 and 7, seem dull and lacking in either narrative drive or spiritual nourishment. Faced with this, many preachers focus on the purple passages and neglect the rest of the books.

This is a great loss because, as I hope to show, the books are a unified and powerful whole with a coherent message, and both strong narrative interest and relevant theology. There is a lot of hard work to be done but this will be wonderfully rewarding as we see God working His purpose out with flawed people, bringing His kingdom nearer, and pointing to the day when the true King will come. Our horizons will be expanded and our faith quickened as we look beyond our own little sphere and see God in the sweep of history. Our confidence in His Word will grow as we see that Word raise up and depose kings and empires; we will be able to read this as part of God's story about God, where the best of His servants only make it by grace and where human leadership depends on faithfulness to the Lord.

There are important issues of background to be covered as we approach these books, and we will need to look at such matters as place in the Bible, historical situation, genre and particular problems such as idolatry and judgment. Much of the terrain will be unfamiliar, but if we study diligently under the guidance of the Spirit we shall hear the Master's voice and see His face.

KINGS IN ITS SETTING

The place of Kings in the Bible

Kings is one book and the division is because of the amount of material which can usefully be included in one scroll (if we may compare the sublime to the ridiculous this is also why the present guide is also coming out in two volumes!). Thus we will refer to Kings as 'the book' rather than 'the books'. Its place in the Bible is first of all as a significant part of the Big Story which runs from creation to new creation and, more specifically along with 1 and 2 Samuel, a history first of the united monarchy and then the divided kingdoms: the northern kingdom of Israel which fell to Assyria in 722 B.C. and the southern kingdom of Judah which was taken into exile in Babylon in 587 B.C. But the first hint of the story of the monarchy comes much earlier when God promises to Abraham (Gen. 17:6) and repeats to Jacob (Gen. 35:11) that kings would come from them. So this story is part of the promises to the patriarchs and points forward to the King who is to come (more on this later).

One other point to notice is that while we call Kings a history book (and it is not less than that), in the Hebrew Bible, the books of Joshua to 2 Kings (except for Ruth) are called 'the former prophets'. This is an important clue as to how we are to look at these books. We will consider this in more detail later, but this emphasis is seen in the large amount of space given to prophets, especially Elijah and Elisha and the way history is seen as God unfolding His purpose.

Kings and history

One of the things which daunts preachers is the length of the book. That, however, should not be exaggerated. The book of Kings in Eugene Peterson's *The Message*[1] runs to only 105 pages. That is not a lot in which to cover nearly 500 years. Imagine compressing the history of Britain from the reign of Elizabeth I to the reign of Elizabeth II into a book as short as that! So the first point to make is that the history is ruthlessly selective, and we shall see examples as we work our way through the book (for example, Omri, Ahab's father is dismissed in six verses, 1 Kings 16:23-28, although we know that he was a big player on the international stage and impressed the Assyrians).

We also need to note that the book is no mere chronicle of events but a record of the living God active in history. This is important as we try to apply the book. We ourselves are not David (or Solomon, or Josiah, and so on) but we have their God. What God writes large on the pages of

---

1. Peterson, E., *The Message* (Carol Stream, US: NavPress, 1993)

history reveals the kind of God He is, and thus how He is to be worshipped and obeyed. What Paul says, speaking specifically of Numbers, 'these things occurred as examples to keep us from setting our hearts on evil things as they did' (1 Cor. 10:6) applies to the rest of the Old Testament. Indeed, since Paul goes on to speak particularly about idolatry, the relevance to Kings is obvious. Thus, while in Kings we are meeting people who actually lived and reading about events which actually happened, we are not taking an antiquarian interest in the book. We are seeing windows into God's purposes and learning how to live lives which honour Him in the present world as we wait for the kingdom.

Thus we shall look at each section in its context but link these with the wider picture as it points to Christ and more will be said of this later in the introduction. This is a book which will lead us to pray 'your kingdom come, your will be done on earth as it is in heaven'.

The book begins with David at the end of his life and continues with a glimpse of glory days under Solomon but this glory fades rapidly before the end of his reign and the kingdom is soon split under his foolish son Rehoboam. The northern kingdom lapses entirely into idolatry and much of the southern kingdom's story is similar, punctuated by a number of relatively good kings such as Asa and Jehoshaphat and two notable Davidic kings, Hezekiah and Josiah, but exile in Babylon looms and Zion mourns. Both kings are talked about in terms which specifically recall David. Hezekiah 'did what was right in the eyes of the LORD just as David his father had done' (2 Kings 18:3). Josiah 'did what was right in the eyes of the LORD and walked in all the ways of his father David' (2 Kings 22:2).

So what is the book about? Can we find a theme which unites the disparate material and which helps us to set about teaching it?

The theme of Kings

Early in the book (1 Kings 2:2-4) we find, I believe, the key which will unlock the riches of the book.

> 'I am about to go the way of all the earth,' he said. 'So be strong, show yourself a man, and observe what the LORD your God requires: Walk in his ways, and keep his decrees and commands, his laws and requirements, as written in the Law of Moses, so that you may prosper in all you do and wherever you go, and that the LORD may keep his promise to me: "If your descendants watch how they live, and if they walk faithfully before me with all their heart and soul, you will never fail to have a man on the throne of Israel."'

These are David's words to Solomon as David bows out. The supreme authority of the words of Moses, which are the words of God, is to be the charter of the kingdom for both king and subjects. We might suggest that the book's theme could be expressed as 'ruling justly and wisely depends on obeying God's Word and this is not only true of the kings but of the people; disobedience is deadly'. The people cannot lead but they can choose to follow or not follow the Word of God. B oth Hezekiah and Josiah were faithful to the Word of God but their reformations were dismantled after their deaths and the whole nation reverted to paganism.

This emphasis is underlined throughout the book with the Word of God coming through many named and

unnamed prophets. The great central section of the book
(1 Kings 17 – 2 Kings 13) is dominated by the ministries
of Elijah and Elisha. Jonah is mentioned in 2 Kings 14:25.
Isaiah plays a prominent role in 2 Kings 18 and 19. The great
reforms of Josiah are given new impetus by the discovery of
the Book of the Law (2 Kings 22:8). The exile is attributed
to disobeying the prophetic Word (2 Kings 24:2-3).

Unpacking this a bit more, we can see how the Word of
promise and rebuke binds the book together. The Word of
God covers the whole of life but there are particular ways
in which this theme is specifically treated in Kings. Three
issues in particular deserve to be mentioned.

The Davidic King

The bookends of Kings draw attention to both the
vulnerability of David's house and the enduring promise
which sustains it. At the beginning of the book, David
lies weak and decrepit, but with the help of Nathan and
Bathsheba, rallies and secures the succession of Solomon
and speaks to him the words already noted (2:2-4) about
the future of the kingdom depending on obedience. At
the end of the book (2 Kings 25:27), the Davidic king
Jehoiachin is raised from prison to sit in a seat of honour
at the table of the Babylonian king. That may be a long way
from the kings of the earth honouring the Son of David but
it is a light in a dark place. Zion is down but not out.

Throughout the book there is constant reference to the
promise to David: the covenant with David of 2 Samuel 7
and Psalm 89. The references are multiple: 1 Kings 11:32;
15:4; 2 Kings 8:19; 20:6 are examples. These, coupled
with the frequent references to the city of David and the
commendation of Hezekiah (2 Kings 18:3) and Josiah

(2 Kings 22:2) for walking in the ways of David, show Yahweh's continuing favour to David's house. Also they point to His Greater Son (a subject we will return to shortly).

The prophetic Word

As already mentioned, the story is punctuated by frequent references to the prophetic Word, both in judgment and salvation. It would be tedious simply to give a list of references and a couple of examples will suffice. Six chapters (1 Kings 17-22) are given to Ahab and the prophetic Word to him from Elijah, Micaiah and an unnamed prophet. These are words of judgment on Ahab and his house for idolatry, but all through the section there is the call to repent. Indeed when Ahab partially responds after his murder of Naboth and the grabbing of his vineyard (1 Kings 21:28-29), Yahweh delays the judgment. In chapter 22:19-23, the false words of the court prophets are attributed to a lying spirit, but it is the words of the true prophet Micaiah which show reality.

Another example of the power of the prophetic Word to save the godly and overthrow kingdoms occurs in 2 Kings 19. The Assyrian spokesman has boasted of the power of Sennacherib. His words are defied by Isaiah, who retorts with the Word of Yahweh (vv. 21-28) and the great Assyrian army is destroyed. Plainly the power of the Word is at the heart of the story.

God's providence and human responsibility

In the unfolding drama of Kings, the responsibility to respond to the Word is central. The Word cannot be broken but human beings are not puppets, as we have already seen in the case of Ahab. The preaching of judgment is in fact a sign of God's grace because it calls for repentance and faith. A clear example of this is 1 Kings 11:29-39, where the prophet Ahijah speaks to Jeroboam, using an acted parable of tearing his cloak into twelve pieces and giving ten of these to Jeroboam to symbolise the ten northern tribes of whom he is shortly to become king. Two tribes remain to the royal house of Judah because of the promise to David. Ahijah promises Jeroboam an enduring royal house as well (v. 38) but that promise depends on Jeroboam's obedience. Jeroboam is hardly crowned when he shows his faithlessness (12:28ff) and judgment is announced (14:6-12).

This emphasis of the challenge of the prophetic Word continues, and even good kings like Hezekiah are judged if they turn to expediency and dangerous alliances rather than follow the path of simple obedience (2 Kings 20:16-18). This pattern of God speaking and humans responsible for hearing and acting is part of the great value of the book. It is of immense practical significance and we shall look at this further as we explore the possibilities of preaching and teaching the book. The important thing is that the Word is living and we cannot simply treat it with indifference.

Structure

Taking it as a unified work one possible approach would be to see six main sections with further subdivisions:

1. Solomon's glory and disgrace (1 Kings 1:1–11:43).
    Solomon is an ambiguous figure and we shall
    explore this in the commentary.

    a. David bows out and Solomon succeeds to
        the throne (1:1–2:46). Here we see human
        vulnerability and divine promise.

    b. Wisdom in wise government (3:1–4:34).
        Solomon at his best gives us a glimpse of the
        kingdom to come.

    c. Building projects (5:1–9:9): temple, palace and
        cities. The high water mark comes at 8:27–30.

    d. National and international activities (9:10–
        10:29) including the memorable visit of the
        Queen of Sheba.

    e. Ending badly (11:1–43). Solomon displays the
        tragedy of divided heart.

2. A dismal bunch of kings (1 Kings 12:1–16:34)

    a. Bad in both north and south (12:1–14:31).
        There is a lot of prophetic activity, especially in
        chapter 13.

    b. Decline in Israel; better things in Judah (15:1–
        16:20), especially seen in the reign of Asa.

    c. Worse still (16:21–34). The house of Omri
        leads Israel to new depths.

3. Bringing God's Word in dangerous times (1 Kings
    17:1 – 2 Kings 13:21); the stories of Elijah and
    Elisha. There is more in this long central section

than the ministry of the two prophets but they dominate this part of the book.

a.   Elijah and Yahweh's powerful protection (17:1–19:21). God protects Elijah and shows the power of His Word.

b.   Ahab confronted by the prophetic Word (20:1–22:41). Ahab is given chance after chance.

c.   Elijah's continuing ministry and his ascension to heaven and Elisha comes into prominence (2 Kings 1:1–2:25).

d.   Elisha's words and actions (2 Kings 3:1–9:13). These are both on the political stage and in private.

e.   More politics (2 Kings 9:14–13:13). Jehu destroys house of Ahab; Athaliah tries to destroy house of David; Joash half-heartedly repairs the temple.

f.   Elisha dies but brings life (2 Kings 13:14-21).

4.   More bad kings (2 Kings 14:22–17:41)

a.   Little to choose between Israel and Judah (14:22–15:38). Israel continues its downward spiral – things are only slightly better in Judah (16).

b.   Goodbye Israel (17:1-41). The northern kingdom is exiled to Assyria and we see why this happened.

5.   Reformers and wreckers (18:1–23:30). We see the two best kings since David but also the worst.

    a.   David comes again (18–20). Hezekiah stands up to the Assyrian Goliath but succumbs to flattery – like David he is flawed but faithful.

    b.   Judah's Ahab (21:1-18). Manesseh is the worst of all the kings. His behaviour makes exile inevitable; a footnote (vv. 19-26) talks of his equally godless son, Amon.

    c.   The Word of Yahweh honoured (22:1–23:30). Josiah's great reformation comes too late to save the nation and he loses his life in an unwise battle with the Pharaoh.

6.   Zion down but not out (23:31–25:30). These are the last dismal days of Judah leading to inevitable exile – but there is a hint of hope for David's line (25:27–30).

A much simpler outline would be to see three main sections:

1.   The glimpse of glory (1 Kings 1–11)

2.   The divided kingdom (1 Kings 12 – 2 Kings 17)

3.   The closing years of Judah (2 Kings 18–25)

It is important that we do not impose a straightjacket on such diverse material, but, as we shall explore further in the section on planning a series, it is important to divide the book into manageable chunks for teaching and preaching. The weakness coupled with the divine protection of the Davidic house that begins and ends the book gives the guiding thread of promise and fulfilment.

It is also important with narrative to read large enough chunks to get the flow of the story as a whole, as well as to see how the smaller units fit into the larger narrative. We will explore the teaching of narrative further in the section on planning a series, but it is important to remember that genre is vitally important.

Context

The place of Kings in the Big Story, beginning with the promise of kings to Abraham (Gen. 17:6) and Jacob (Gen. 35:11), has already been noted, as has the significance of David and his sons. The apparent eclipse of that promise at the Exile is gloriously transformed with the words of Gabriel announcing the birth of great David's Greater Son 'the Lord God will give him the throne of his father David, and he will reign over the house of Jacob forever' (Luke 1:33). Paul, in Rom 15:12, speaks of the Davidic King reigning over the nations as the Gentiles gather to Christ. In Revelation, the 'Lion of the tribe of Judah, the root of David' opens the scroll of history (5:5). In Rev. 22:16 he is the origin and also the offspring of David.

However, there is one book which invites specific comparison with Kings and that is Chronicles (like Kings, one book but divided for convenience into two scrolls). Both cover similar ground but with different emphases. Kings shows why the exile happened, whereas Chronicles is written to encourage the remnant who returned from exile to see themselves in direct continuity with Moses and David as the covenant people whom God would continue to bless.

Thus in Chronicles many of David and Solomon's failures are omitted in order to emphasise their positive achievements as the foundation of Israel's hopes. The Chronicler particularly emphasises the extensive role

of David in planning and providing for the work of the
Temple (1 Chron. 22–27) as well as the orderly transfer
of power from David to Solomon (1 Chron. 28-29). There
is also far more extensive coverage of many of the kings of
Judah in Chronicles: e.g. Jehoshaphat, the weak man who
nevertheless trusted God in a crisis (2 Chron. 20); Uzziah the
strong man discredited because of his pride (2 Chron. 26);
the religious reforms of Hezekiah (2 Chron. 30-31); the
belated repentance of Manasseh which failed to avert the
Exile (2 Chron. 33).

The books of Kings and Chronicles complement each
other but their theology of a God who saves and judges is
common to both. The genealogies which open Chronicles
are a reminder of God's care for all His people and their
personal importance to Him. Likewise the glories of David
and Solomon anticipate the greater glory of the King who
is to come.

It is important when we are preaching on Kings not to
import too much material from Chronicles but to focus on
the particular emphases of the author. Otherwise we shall
end up preaching a mishmash which does not do justice
to either book, rather like some sermons on the Gospels
which take an incident such as the Feeding of the Five
Thousand and preach a hybrid sermon which does not do
justice to the emphases of any of the particular Gospels.
We must avoid such homogenisation.

An example of this would be the treatment of
Jehoshaphat. In 1 Kings 22 – 2 Kings 3 he appears as
an associate of Ahab and then Jehoram. His reforms are
not ignored (1 Kings 22:41-50) but the author's emphasis
is on his unwise cosying up to Ahab's house. Kings does
not deny that he was a good man but shows how he failed

to realise his potential. Chronicles, while recognising his weakness, contains more detailed treatment of his reforms and especially his faith (in 2 Chron. 20) when he is faced with a vast army. Each book is contributing to the total picture but we need to stick to the text in front of us. We can mention the differences but not major on them.

Authorship

The book itself gives no hint about who wrote it; the evidence of unified themes and careful planning suggests a single author. It was long believed that this was Jeremiah, not just because of the identical endings of the books (2 Kings 25 and Jer. 52) but because of a similarity in outlook and theology, not least the extensive treatment of the Word of Yahweh. Clearly it cannot have been earlier than about 560 B.C., given the reference to Jehoiachin at the end of the book.

Obviously the author used sources such as royal annals, temple records and stories passed down in prophetic circles. The important thing is that this book is part of Scripture and is profitable whosoever the human author may have been.

WHY SHOULD WE PREACH
AND TEACH 2 KINGS?

We can dodge this important issue and say, in effect, we have to preach it because it is there. Naturally, if we are committed to preaching the whole Bible we will preach on Kings as well as every other part. But more specifically, what is there about the book that makes its own unique contribution to the canon and makes it profitable as we follow the Lord? Four reasons can be given to help us to unpack the riches of this book.

Kings is God's story about God

One of the ways in which narrative works (see section on preaching narrative p. 47ff) is by presenting truth indirectly as well as directly. What I mean is that in the narrative, without specific comment, the author shows us the nature, activities and ways of God by the flow of the story itself. Thus the cluster of Elijah stories in chapters 17 – 19 of 1 Kings, apart from the specific attack on idolatry, show us important truths about God in the way the narrative progresses. Thus we learn that He cares about physical needs and can supply these in unexpected ways (ravens

and a widow in 17:6, 14; an angel in 19:5-7). He answers
not fanatical ravings and hype, but simple, heartfelt prayer
(18:27-29; 36-7). He does not dump His faithful servants
on the scrapheap but allows them to rest and then gives
them new tasks to do (19:5-8; 15-18).

Also, God's care for ordinary, often nameless, people
is powerfully brought out in a chapter such as 2 Kings 4.
There, those who receive the Lord's blessing through Elisha
are otherwise unknown. That is not, of course, confined
to this chapter: the wise treatment of the prostitutes by
Solomon (1 Kings 3:16-28); the lepers in 2 Kings 7:9; the
concern of Hezekiah for the ordinary citizens as they hear
the Assyrian boasts (2 Kings 18:36) show similar emphasis.

There is also the activity of God in the events of history.
He raises up kings against Solomon (1 Kings 11:23);
controls events (1 Kings 12:15); removes His people to
exile when they rebel against Him (2 Kings 17:20-23;
23:27). He acts in judgment: death by fire (2 Kings 1:12).
He acts in mercy as the One who hears and answers prayer
(for Elijah in 1 Kings 18:36-38; for Hezekiah in 2 Kings
19:14-19). Many similar examples could be cited, but these
will suffice to show how awesome and gracious is the God
of Kings.

In today's world these are truths which need to be
preached over and over again. Too often in pursuit of trying
to deal with felt needs, we strive for a superficial relevance
rather than allowing these great truths about God to fill
our hearts and stretch our minds. Often, we offer a tame
domesticated God whose main function is to make us feel
comfortable and offer quick fixes to deep-rooted problems.
We need a God who can handle the giant evils of the world
to all who repent.

This book will point to God-centred preaching which is vital in the building of God-centred congregations and which will encourage faith in God's promises and obedience to God's Word. Since this is narrative these great truths about God are embodied in real people and situations and this brings us to our next reason for preaching Kings.

Kings tells us about the kingdom of God

When we pray 'your kingdom come, your will be done on earth as it is in heaven', we know that prayer will only ultimately be fulfilled when the King returns and ushers in the new heaven and the new earth. However, it is also a prayer for that kingdom to be anticipated in our lives, both communal and personal. We also know only too well that values which are not kingdom values often predominate. Here in Kings (as in Samuel) we have a visual aid of an earthly kingdom which points to the future. This is an important point: at various times this small earthly kingdom was a genuine anticipation of the kingdom of our God and His Christ.

Unsurprisingly, the clearest glimpses of the kingdom come from the early and middle years of Solomon when the nation was united. The unity of God's people remains an important Biblical truth (John 17:22). But there are other important glimpses of how, even on earth, the kingdom is anticipated. In 1 Kings 3:7-15, the kingdom is strongest when the king rules with God-given wisdom. We are not Solomon, but those in pastoral oversight need wisdom and the mind of Christ through listening to Him in His Word, and by His Spirit applying that Word both to ourselves and then others. The story of the two prostitutes (3:16-28) shows that such rule is marked by compassion and a shrewd understanding of human nature.

1 Kings 4 also shows wise administration of the kingdom and the fulfilment of the prophecy to Abraham in Gen. 15:18 that the kingdom would stretch from the Nile to the Euphrates. These territories had been conquered by David (see 2 Sam. 8). Further wisdom involves intellectual, imaginative and aesthetic pleasure in God's creation. These emphases give a rich and rounded picture of human life, partial here but fully realised in the new creation. Teaching such truths will help to avoid super-spirituality which denies the good gifts God has given us in this present life and has an unattractive and disembodied view of the new creation.

The next few chapters (5-8) show the genuine worship of the kingdom in the loving care lavished on the building of the temple. This is not to be pressed into service to prop up an ailing fabric fund. This is ultimately about building living stones in the temple of God's people: God's people in the OT were an anticipation of the new creation. The high water mark is 8:27-30 where Solomon worships the Lord who is both enthroned in the highest heaven but condescends to come into time and space. As any serious Bible student will be able to tell you the key to Biblical theology is God up there (Gen. 1) who comes down here (Gen. 2), pointing to the perfect union of the new heaven and earth (Rev. 21:1-4).

There are other glimpses of the kingdom later in the book, not least in the godly fellowship of the prophets (I will come to this shortly). However, even in days of decline, good things happen. Asa of Judah removes idolatrous practices in face of strong family opposition (1 Kings 15:11-14) a policy followed by his son Jehoshaphat (1 Kings 22:43). Jehosheba hides the young Joash, thereby saving the Davidic line (2 Kings 11:1-3). Hezekiah gives a glimpse of the Davidic kingdom, including defying the Assyrian Goliath (2 Kings 18–19). Josiah makes a valiant effort to reinstate the Word of God at the centre of national life (2 Kings 22–23).

The kingdom is under persistent attack and this is the other side of the same coin: there is much to learn about this from Kings. We do not have to choose between focussing on the big picture of the kingdom and the ethical imperatives of that kingdom. To preserve the sheep we have to fight the wolf; to live according to kingdom principles we have to fight the enemies of the kingdom.

So, as we teach Kings we will need to present the negatives as well as the positives. At the heart of Kings is the warning expressed by John at the end of his first letter 'Dear children, keep yourselves from idols' (1 John 5:21). This perpetual temptation to build a visible kingdom which ultimately we can manipulate is first disastrously seen in the great Solomon himself (1 Kings 11:1-8). The whole sorry story continues to exile because once Yahweh becomes simply another god-let, the distinctive kingdom lifestyle disappears. As we preach and teach this we need to examine our own idolatries, not least our evangelical ones: the celebrity culture; the obsession with numbers; the excessive busyness and the like. Each of us is in different situations with different idolatries. We also need to deal with the idols in our own hearts and it is surely significant that Solomon's idolatry was traced to his heart (1 Kings 11:4, 9).

Kings tells us about the Word of God

The book is dominated by the centrality of the Word of God which saves and judges. This is established by David's last words to Solomon (1 Kings 2:2-4) and continued in the prophetic ministries of the great and the unknown; it culminates in the great reforms of Josiah (2 Kings 22 & 23). One thing this does is help to create and sustain confidence in the Word of God to do its work. This is a Word which 'will not return empty... but achieve the purpose for which I sent it' (Isa. 55:11). We see this over and over again in the narrative of Kings.

We are not prophets, but we have been given the prophetic Word which as Peter says is 'a light shining in a dark place' (2 Pet. 1:19). At significant crisis points, prophets are involved bringing the Word of God into the situation: Nathan in the accession of Solomon (1 Kings 1:22); Ahijah announcing the divided kingdom (1 Kings 11:29-39; 14:1-18); Elijah to the house of Omri (1 Kings 17 – 2 Kings 1) and Isaiah to Hezekiah (2 Kings 19:20-34). That does not mean that we can look at the politics of today and give authoritative messages to prime ministers and presidents as if we had God-given authority to pronounce on government policies. Rather, the general principles of a worldview flowing from a God of justice and mercy are the foundation of truly biblical living and God-fearing community.

The Word of God is more important than the messenger who brings it and it is a Word of challenge in the present which shapes the future. It is encouraging to see how the Word is not bound by time; a striking example of this is when the man of God from Judah prophesies to Jeroboam about how one day a Davidic king called Josiah will cleanse the land from idolatry (1 Kings 13:2-3). As we preach and teach we understandably like to see fruit from our labours and often God generously gives that. However, that Word spoken and apparently opposed or ignored may bear a harvest long after we have gone.

Kings points to Christ

Preachers are often unsure about how to see appropriate lines to Christ, and one reason for the neglect of much of the Old Testament is that many find it hard to see Christ in the text. Thus there may be a sermon on Esther which could have been preached in the synagogue followed by some lame statement like 'it's really all about Jesus'. At this point the hearers may legitimately scratch their heads and think 'Did I miss something?'. Or else the OT passage may simply be used as a springboard to jump into the New Testament. Thus a sermon, allegedly on Isaiah 53, is in effect a sermon on Acts 8. However, we need to remember that the apostles and other preachers in the early decades preached from the 'Scriptures' by which, like the risen Lord on the way to Emmaus (Luke 24:27), they meant what we call the Old Testament.

At first sight Kings does not seem to be the most promising book from which to proclaim Christ, but if we take seriously the points already made about the nature of God and the kingdom, quite a different picture begins to emerge. The starting point is the emphasis on David and the Davidic dynasty. Neither David himself, nor even the most deserving of his sons, truly ruled over a kingdom whose throne was established forever (see 2 Sam. 7:13). Yet, as already noticed, there are tantalising glimpses of

that kingdom and while in the northern kingdom, four
dynasties rise and fall, the house of David persists to the
Exile and beyond. Even in human terms, 500 years is a long
time for a royal house to survive.

Thus, in spite of the failures of the human kings, the
hope still burns that one day there will be a son of David
who will embody the covenant and fulfil all its promises.
This is already implied in the words of Ahijah to Jeroboam
that David's descendants would be humbled but not
forever (1 Kings 11:39). Even Exile did not break the line of
promise. The Davidic king, Jehoiachin, in exile in Babylon
is raised to the highest place at the king of Babylon's table
(2 Kings 25:27-30). This points to the day when the King
reigns on the holy hill of Zion.

The reigns of the better kings, as already noticed, point
to the time when David's Greater Son will reign over the
whole of creation. But on the other hand the reigns of the
bad kings point to the need for the true king who will reign
in righteousness and peace. Idolatry and apostasy brought
nothing but misery, tyranny and endless wars, and showed
starkly the need for a different kind of kingdom. The
words of David to Solomon (2:2-4) not only emphasise the
centrality of the words of Moses but the vital importance
of a son of the Davidic line who would embody their truth.

Kings is a vital stage in the journey which is to lead to
the announcement to Mary by Gabriel that the Saviour
to be born was the One to whom 'the Lord God will
give the throne of his father David, and he will reign
over the house of Jacob for ever; his kingdom will never
end' (Luke 1:32-33). The phrase 'house of Jacob' neatly
sums up the book of Kings, as that name reminds us of

all the waywardness and sinfulness of the people as God's abundant grace transforms Jacob into Israel.

Similarly, Jesus is the true Prophet to whom all the prophetic figures in Kings point. But He is also the true Word, not simply the One who brings that Word. It was from the book of Kings that He spoke in His first synagogue sermon, speaking of the grace of God to Gentile widows and lepers (Luke 4:24-27). And there He was the object of hatred that is so often the lot of the true prophet.

Preaching Christ from Kings is not an alien construct imposed on the text but rises naturally and inevitably from it. Different preachers will tackle these issues in different ways and we need to be sensitive and not over-allegorise, for example, the details of the temple furnishings, but our task is faithfully to proclaim the living Word as He appears in the pages of the written Word. As we preach Christ it is not so much having a checklist imposed on every passage as developing an ear to hear the Master's voice.

At various points in the commentary, I will pause to consider the question of how we preach Christ faithfully from the text. The aim of these sections attached to clusters of chapters, rather than individual ones, is to underline that our purpose in preaching is never simply to 'explain the passage' as if it were a mere exercise in comprehension but to proclaim Christ who is the great centre of the Bible. This is not simply in terms of His earthly life but His eternal being and activity throughout history and the eternal kingdom. Not every passage or even every book will focus on all these aspects and in Kings especially His kingship and His role as the great Prophet and occasionally the Priest will be emphasised.

Preaching Old Testament Narrative

Kings is part of the great narrative of the Bible which begins with creation and culminates in the new creation and, as we preach it, we need to consider how we can handle narrative effectively. This is worth some brief consideration before we get to the text itself. The first thing that needs to be said is that, if we believe that God gave us the Bible, then *how* He says something will be a vital part of *what* He says. Thus we will not preach narrative as if it was a doctrinal passage. We will be primarily interested in how God's story about God embodies the Gospel.

So what are the characteristics of narrative and how can we avoid moralising platitudes which is a constant danger in preaching story? First we must remember these are, in many cases, exciting and gripping stories, and we need to enjoy reading them as we would any other good story. Not all of Kings is narrative of that kind and, as we go through the exposition, we will consider the place and value of such passages as the long temple-building section (1 Kings 5–7) and the brief notes on the inglorious reigns of insignificant kings (e.g. 2 Kings 14 and 15). However, we need to be absorbed in the flow of the story and the place of individual episodes in the great narrative.

OT narrative, like any other story, has a number of components which together create the text. It is not a case of simply isolating these elements so much as seeing how together they create the story as we have it.

Plot is the first major part of story: the sequence of events, including principles of selection and the silences of the text. For example in Kings, the author gives a brief summary of the sequence of kings in 1 Kings 15 and 16 concluding with Ahab and we expect he will be dismissed in a few verses like his predecessors. However, the account of his reign spans chapters 17–22 because it is to be the backdrop to the ministry of Elijah and others, and to underline the supreme importance of the prophetic Word. Hezekiah's religious reforms are given one verse (2 Kings 18:4) because again the emphasis is on the prophetic Word brought by Isaiah. As we preach the individual stories we will also notice the structure of the narrative and how the author's emphases are shown within episodes as well as the wider balance in the book as a whole.

Characterisation is another important element in story. God is the main actor but the part played by humans matters, hence the frequent references to David. Sometimes these characters will be developed at some length, notably Solomon. If the interpretation of Solomon in this book is accepted then we have a more convincing human being than if we see him as virtually flawless from 1 Kings 2-10 and then suddenly and without warning falling from grace in chapter 11. However it is not just the big players but the 'little' people who are vital in God's purpose, for example the little girl who told Naaman's wife about Elisha in 2 Kings 5:3 and the unnamed prophet who anointed Jehu in 2 Kings 9:6. Very often dialogue develops characterisation as in 1 Kings 1 and 2 where Solomon emerges as king.

Setting is important and often draws attention to deeper elements in the story. Warning bells ring in 1 Kings 10 at the elaborate luxury and extravagance of Solomon's court (compare a similar technique in Esther 1 regarding the Persian court). Also the significance of Mount Carmel in 1 Kings 18 which emphasises that this contest of Yahweh and Baal is happening on Baal's home ground; if he cannot win here he cannot win anywhere.

Application needs to be considered carefully. Narrative is not normative: for example, 'David did well, so imitate him'; 'David did badly, so don't imitate him'. However, in a legitimate desire to avoid this kind of moralising, there has developed a tendency to flatten out every narrative in terms of the big picture. This results in very repetitive preaching where virtually the same thing is said every week. Also, a commendable desire to avoid moralising has led to a neglecting of the 'so what?' There are implications for our lives and Paul sets this out clearly in 1 Corinthians 10:1ff. These will follow from close exegesis of the text and showing not only the big picture but showing how particular passages bring their own contribution to it.

Above all we are not following a formula, we are developing an instinct for seeing each part of the Bible and each genre making their own unique contributions to the developing story. Kings speaks of a vital time in the history of God's people when they declined from the glory days of David and Solomon to bitter exile. Along the route

prophets warned them, some good kings tried to stop the
rot, but the dream ended in apparent failure. Yet, as we
shall see at the end of the book in 2 Kings 25:27-30, there
is hope beyond despair. We are part of that story and so the
story speaks to us.

LIST OF KINGS OF ISRAEL

(Dates of reigns are B.C. and all approximate)

THE UNITED KINGDOM			
Saul	1050-1010		
David	1010-970		
Solomon	970-930		
THE DIVIDED KINGDOM			
Kings of Judah		Kings of Israel	
Rehoboam 931-913	1 Kings 11:43	Jeroboam I 931-910	1 Kings 11:31
Abijah 913-911	1 Kings 14:31	Nadab 910-909	1 Kings 14:20
Asa 911-870	1 Kings 15:8	Baasha 909-886	1 Kings 15:16
Jehoshaphat 870-848	1 Kings 15:24	Elah 886-885	1 Kings 16:8
J[eh]oram 848-841	2 Kings 8:16	Zimri 885	1 Kings 16:15

Ahaziah 841	2 Kings 8:25	Omri 885-874	1 Kings 16:16
Qu. Athaliah 841-835	2 Kings 8:26	Ahab 874-853	1 Kings 16:29
J[eh]oash 835-796	2 Kings 11:2	Ahaziah 853-852	1 Kings 22:40
Amaziah 796-767	2 Kings 14:1	J[eh]oram 852-841	2 Kings 1:17
Azariah 767-740	2 Kings 14:21	Jehu 841-814	2 Kings 9:1
Jotham 740-732	2 Kings 15:32	Jehoahaz 814-798	2 Kings 10:35
Ahaz 732-716	2 Kings 15:38	Jehoash 798-782	2 Kings 13:10
Hezekiah 716-687	2 Kings 16:20	Jeroboam II 782-753	2 Kings 14:23
Manasseh 687-642	2 Kings 21:1	Zechariah 753-752	2 Kings 14:29
Amon 642-640	2 Kings 21:19	Shallum 752	2 Kings 15:10
Josiah 640-608	2 Kings 22:1	Menahem 752-742	2 Kings 15:14
Jehoahaz 608	2 Kings 23:30	Pekahiah 742-740	2 Kings 15:23
Jehoiakim 608-597	2 Kings 23:34	Pekah 740-732	2 Kings 15:25
Jehoiachin 597	2 Kings 24:6	Hoshea 732-712	2 Kings 15:30
Zedekiah 597-586	2 Kings 24:17	Fall of Samaria 722 B.C.	
Fall of Jerusalem 586 B.C.			

Reading Long Narrative Passages

Alec Motyer used to remind preachers that the only inspired words they would say would be while they read the Biblical passage. That is an important reminder that the public reading of Scripture is not the curtain raiser to the main act but the most significant moment when the voice of God comes to us. That applies not just to narrative but there are particular difficulties involved in reading long chunks of narrative in an age more attuned to sound bites. Yet we owe it to the Lord and to our hearers to do it as well as possible and to give our minds and hearts to it.

Perhaps it might be useful to take a particular long narrative as an illustration of how this might work. The story in question is the attack on Judah by Sennacherib, king of Assyria and the threat to Jerusalem itself. The narrative runs continuously from 2 Kings 18:17 to 2 Kings 19:37, fifty-two verses in all, but it is a coherent narrative and the tension and excitement build up through it and these would be missed if we only reads extracts.

One practical point is to split the narrative in two and have a hymn between the readings. It is important if we do this that we have an appropriate place to break off and in a narrative like this a cliffhanger would be appropriate. My suggestion is to read from 18:17 to 19:13 still a longish but manageable reading, breaking off at the point where Sennacherib has sent a letter full of blood-curdling threat to Hezekiah. It is also important to choose an appropriate hymn to help to crystallise the message, one which expresses trust as well as fear. Perhaps something like 'My times are in your hand' or 'Our confidence is in the Lord'.

Getting back to the actual reading of the Kings passage we notice that much of it is dialogue and direct speech which ought to be reflected when reading aloud. The Assyrian commander's first speech (18:19-25) is sarcastic and condescending and that tone needs to be reflected. His second speech (18:28-35) has some of that but he also uses insincere and plausible speech (31-32). Hezekiah's words to his official which they report to Isaiah (19:3-4) have the tone of penitence as well as hope. Isaiah's reply (19:5-7) is brisk and no-nonsense. Hezekiah's prayer is earnest (19:15-19) and I do not mean using a 'holy whine' voice but being fully conscious of the serious situation he faces and even more of the greatness of God. Isaiah's reply is full of vigorous confidence as well as real encouragement (19:20-34). All these different tones will be reflected in a good reading.

This means that here and elsewhere we need to immerse ourselves in the stories: reflect the flow of the narrative, noting where it speeds up and slows down; entering imaginatively the world of the characters and helping listeners grasp how the story develops. Part of this is timing, knowing when to pause and when to read more quickly. A good reading will be the best possible preparation for people to look forward eagerly to the exposition. A few words (no more) to put the narrative in context are always helpful.

The question as to *who* does the reading is up to the individual leader to decide. Some argue that the person preaching has studied the passage and is therefore the best person to read it effectively. There is truth in that but it is not an absolute. What must be emphasised is the importance of the passage being read well to show we are subject to its authority.

Part 2:

The Divided Kingdom
Cont. (2 Kings 1–17)

I

THE WORD OF THE TRUE GOD (I)

Introduction

As already noted in the introductory material there is no break in narrative between the end of 1 Kings and the beginning of 2 Kings; the division is because of what can be contained in one scroll. The idolatry in Israel continues unchecked, indeed if anything gets worse, as Ahab's son Ahaziah brings to a crescendo the evil ways of both his parents as well as echoing those of that first notorious idolater, Jeroboam son of Nebat. The only mercy of this evil reign was that it lasted a mere two years (1 Kings 22:51-53). The author here gives us a flavour of that inglorious time by concentrating on the episode which brings about Ahaziah's death.

More significantly the powerful ministry of Elijah occupies centre stage. I argued in the exposition of 1 Kings chapter 19 (in the previous volume) that the interpretation of that chapter which virtually writes him off as a spent force cannot be sustained and we saw how the episode of

Naboth's vineyard (1 Kings 21) already gives the lie to that. Here this chapter and the next confirm that to the end Elijah remains a force for God challenging godless kings and bringing the powerful Word of God.

There is a close parallel between this episode and 1 Kings 18 as on both occasions fire falls from heaven to show who the true God is and to authenticate His genuine servant. The difference is that in 1 Kings 18 the fire is a call to repentance and faith, here it is an act of judgment. Ahaziah and his first two captains do not tremble at the Word of God and thus that Word judges them. However, there is grace in the chapter especially in the mercy shown to the third captain (vv. 13-15). In fact this is a chapter about reactions to the Gospel: to Ahaziah it is the stench of death but to the third captain the fragrance of life (2 Cor. 2:15-16). This is the Gospel for today as we proclaim Christ among the multitude of false gods.

Listening to the text

Context and structure

The setting is the aftermath of the death of Ahab, mentioned here in verse 1 and described in 1 Kings 22:34-38. The detail that Moab rebelled is significant. The implication is that Ahab had kept firm control. There may also be an implied contrast with Jehoshaphat of Judah who kept Edom under control (1 Kings 22:47).

The scene is set for the final clash between Elijah and the house of Ahab and more importantly another contest between Yahweh and the pagan gods.

The text can be divided in the following way:

   ✦   Consulting false gods (1:1-2)

+ Who is the true God? (1:3-8)

+ God protects His man (1:9-12)

+ Humility averts judgment (1:13-15)

+ God's Word carried out (1:16-18)

Working through the text

Consulting false gods (1:1-2)

An apparent accident shows where Ahaziah's trust lies as he falls from a top floor and, badly injured, sends his messengers to consult a pagan god. 1 Kings 22:51-53 have shown that this was no unfortunate lapse but a sign of his regular practice. The god in question is Baal-Zebub of Ekron. This Philistine city was the most northerly one, about twenty-five miles north-west of Jerusalem. The god may have been renowned as a healer but if Ahaziah had been familiar with the earlier history of his people he would have known the bad track record of the Philistine gods. Dagan the chief god had been turned into Humpty Dumpty as the Ark of the Covenant had been put in his temple to show his superiority to Yahweh (1 Sam 5:1-5). Goliath had cursed David by his gods (1 Sam 17:43) and much good it did him. The name 'Baal-Zebub' means 'lord of the flies' or the 'dung god' referring to flies buzzing around decaying matter and is almost certainly a deliberate change from 'Baal-Zebul' – 'Baal the exalted'. This is a god of death not of life. Matthew 10:25 uses it as a name of Satan, a reminder of the demonic activity behind pagan idolatry.

Ahaziah sends messengers to 'consult' this futile deity who like all the other manifestations of Baal is to prove impotent. This consultation would be by means of an

oracle, a practice forbidden in Leviticus 19:31. This is
another deliberate flouting of the words of Moses and a
contempt for the prophetic Word which Ahaziah must
have known about.

Who is the true God? (1:3-8)
Ahaziah may have sent his messengers but God now
sends His and Elijah intercepts Ahaziah's men on the
road to Ekron. Such was the authority of Elijah that the
messengers risk the royal anger and return to the king with
a message from God but not the god he had sent them to.
The phrase 'is it because there is no God in Israel?' is a
powerful reminder of 1 Kings 18 and it brings a message
of judgment. Will Ahaziah repent and seek the Lord in
his remaining days? What follows shows that he will not.
Instead he is only curious about who sent the message (v. 7)
and instantly realises that it is Elijah whom he would be
well aware of from his father's reign.

The author does not tell us how he responded to this
news in terms of his inner thoughts although in the next
section we are to see the action he takes. Probably he had
forgotten about Elijah (as Belshazzar forgot about Daniel
[Dan. 5:10-13]) and Ahaziah certainly cannot have been
pleased at this unwelcome reminder of the past.

God protects His man (1:9-12)
What Ahaziah does now shows both his attempt to
intimidate Elijah and also a certain superstitious fear
as he sends a whole detachment to arrest one man. The
foolishness of this is seen when the captain addresses
Elijah as 'man of God', a term which marginalises all
earthly authority. It also shows the stupidity of believing
in pagan gods who might well be manipulated by earthly

powers. Just as the fire from heaven failed to turn Jezebel from her chosen path (see 1 Kings 19:1-2) so the fate of the first detachment does not turn Ahaziah to repentance and he sends a second captain with a second detachment with the same demand and the same result.

This episode has been much criticised for its alleged vindictiveness and Luke 9:54-55 has been used to see what Elijah did here as barbaric. But we must remember first the situation. For many decades now Israel had systematically abandoned the faith of Yahweh, a process accelerated by Ahab and Jezebel and continuing undiminished under Ahaziah. The name and honour of Yahweh were at stake. The king was demanding the kind of allegiance that no human has any right to demand. In any case it was Yahweh who sent the fire not Elijah and therefore we cannot conclude that God felt He had to vindicate His servant publicly although He did not approve of what he did. There is no hint of this in the text and this conclusion calls into question the very character of God. Also Yahweh is protecting His servant and showing he is the same man as the Elijah of Carmel. The Luke passage must be seen in the whole context of the book. Earlier Jesus had read from Isaiah 61:1-2 stopping at 'the year of the Lord's favour' and before 'the day of vengeance of our God' because that had not yet arrived. Here there is an anticipation of that day in the judgment on the military but we are about to see also grace at work.

Humility averts judgment (1:13-15)
Ahaziah has learned nothing and yet again tries brute force. This time, however, the third captain recognises realities and shows proper respect for the man of God. There is

more here than fear for his life; he is obviously more in awe of Elijah and Elijah's God than he is of Ahaziah and for that matter, Baal-Zebub. God alone knows the heart but there is genuine repentance here. The fact that the angel of Yahweh tells Elijah not to be afraid shows that Elijah's life had been in danger. Ahaziah was neither the first nor last person who thought that he could evade the Word of God by killing the messenger.

Fire from heaven had failed to turn Ahaziah to repentance as it had failed with his father and mother. The king had already heard the Word of God but was unwilling to heed it. This meant that unlike the third captain, judgment is inevitable and this is to be the subject of the final section of the chapter.

God's Word carried out (1:16-18)
There comes a time when the Word which is persistently rejected destroys those who oppose it. Here there is to be no deathbed repentance as the Word of judgment already spoken in verse 4 is carried out. Elijah has nothing more to say to Ahaziah and simply repeats that Word which is swiftly carried out. The ominous phrase 'you will certainly die' (vv. 4, 16) is a deliberate echo of Genesis 2:17 and a reminder that this judgment is not unique to Ahaziah but the sentence on all who sin and fall short of the glory of God, which is everyone. Notice the way verse 17 describes why Ahaziah died not because of his injury but 'according to the Word of Yahweh that Elijah had spoken'. Here is yet another confirmation of the power of the Word of God which we have identified as the main theme of Kings as well as another authentication of Elisha's ministry.

Ahaziah's inglorious reign is over but Ahab's house lives on for a time. Yahweh had said to Elijah He would bring disaster in the reign of Ahab's son (1 Kings 21:29). This disaster, to be described in 2 Kings 9, is to happen in the reign of Jehoram or Joram whom we learn in 2 Kings 3:1 is another son of Ahab. Once again we have a brief note that the events of Ahaziah's reign are recorded in the court records of the Israelite kings and once again we are left to reflect how empty these vanished annals are compared with a name written in the book of life.

From text to message

Getting the message clear: the theme
The Word of the true God will always accomplish its purpose no matter the level of opposition. Pagan superstition may have spurious attraction but will be exposed as hollow and impotent.

Getting the message clear: the aim
To increase confidence in the Word of God will be our emphasis in this rather dark chapter and to emphasise that there is a true God among His people even when they have departed from His ways. A further aim would be to show God's faithfulness to His servant in this, Elijah's last public ministry before he is taken to heaven. We need to emphasise that a faithful Word depends on a faithful God.

A way in
We need to alert people to the sinister side of idolatry. One way of doing this would be to refer to William Golding's novel *The Lord of the Flies*, written in 1956 but subsequently a regular text taught in English departments. Many will

therefore have read the novel and more will have seen the film. Essentially a story of a group of polite English public school boys marooned on an island who soon turn into a pack of savages. Evil is both inside and around them and this becomes identified with the lord of the flies, a pig's head on a stake in a forest clearing. There, as here, evil is both internal to the human heart and external to it, and in both the novel and 1 Kings 1 it is represented by the lord of the flies.

Here we need to emphasise the contrast between 'consulting' false gods with all its mumbo jumbo and simple obedience to the clear Word of God. I shall look at this further in ideas for application but it must be central as we teach the passage.

Ideas for application

+   This chapter, like so much in the Ahab and sons' story is an exposure of idolatry and we need to think through exactly what we are going to say. How easy it is to expose the idolatries of others, whether Catholic or liberal or even charismatic. That is safe as well because it can easily lapse into playing to the prejudices of our own circles. The key here is the repeated phrase 'is it because there is no God in Israel?' (vv. 3, 6, 16) and that is where the emphasis must lie. Most of us are not likely to consult Baal-Zebub, the god of Ekron, but this repeated question sharply shows the true nature of idolatry which is where do we turn in a time of crisis? We often lose confidence in the Word of God and use the language and techniques of big business and rely on secular models. These can so easily become more important than humble faithfulness and lead to fellowships which are theoretically evangelical but which are no longer driven by the Word of God.

+ This chapter also highlights the clash of different kinds of power. The first two captains fear the anger of the king. The third captain's faith like Moses' faith (Heb. 11:27) is shown by not fearing the king's anger. So faith is shown by whether we are more afraid of the visible problem or the invisible God.

+ It is also a chapter of Gospel grace particularly to the third captain who shows that repentance leads to rescue from judgment. Ahaziah and his first two captains could have received the same mercy. If we doubt that we need only read Luke 23:40-43 where one of the vilest offenders truly believes and that moment from Jesus a pardon receives.

+ This passage points to Christ the One who has authority over death, demons and disease and whose words not only have power as Elijah's did but is Himself the living Word of God. Also in the figure of the Angel of Yahweh who is both distinct from God but speaks His very words we have a pre-incarnate appearance of Christ. Everything He says is not only true but will come to pass.

Suggestions for preaching

Sermon 1: Which God do you trust?
This would take the repeated question 'is it because there is no God in Israel?' (vv. 3, 6, 16) as a structure for the sermon.

Introduction
Place the story in context of 1 Kings 22:51-53 – continuing line of Ahab.

The true God is faithful
The first time the question is asked (v. 3).

+   His faithfulness in the past – God in Israel rather than, for example, God of heaven, emphasises His blessing of His people.

+   The futility of Philistine gods – see comments in exposition.

The true God is active
The second time the question is asked (v. 6).

+   The fire of judgment – first two captains.

+   The mercy which responds to humility – third captain.

The true God keeps His Word
The third time the question is asked (v. 16).

+   The rejected Word becomes the judging Word.

+   God's servant is vindicated.

Sermon 2
This could focus on the human responses.

Blind unbelief

+   Ahaziah's stubborn defiance.

+   The first two captains' arrogance.

Searching humility

+   Third captain shows trembling before God.

+   He recognises Elijah as true messenger.

Strong confidence

+   Elijah's uncompromising Word.

✦   Elijah's authentification.

Suggestions for teaching

Questions to help understand the passage

1. Why does the author mention Moab's rebellion against Israel?

2. Why are we not surprised that Ahaziah sends for help to a pagan god? (See 1 Kings 22:51-53.)

3. Why did the king's messengers return to him without consulting Baal-Zebub?

4. What does the fire from heaven tell us about Elijah and his message? (Read again 1 Kings 18, especially vv. 22-39.)

5. How does the third captain show genuine humility? (vv. 13-14)

6. Why does Elijah simply repeat the words of the original message? (vv. 3, 6, 16)

7. What is the point of verse 18?

Questions to help apply the passage

1. In what ways might we lapse into idolatry even though we do not consult Baal-Zebub, god of Ekron?

2. The question 'is it because there is no God in Israel?' (v. 3 and repeated in vv. 6 and 16) goes right to the heart of faith. What can we learn about faith and superstition in our own time from this?

3. The fire from heaven recalls 1 Kings 18 and is not something we expect to happen in our day. However it teaches us important things about the nature of God. Outline what some of these are.

4. What does this chapter teach us about the gospel of grace?

5. How does this chapter teach us to persist in preaching the Word? (Look again at the repeated question in verses 3, 6, 16.)

6. In what ways does this chapter point to Christ? You might look at the angel of the LORD (vv. 3, 15); at the triumph of the Word and the defeat of the powers of darkness.

2

The Parting of the Ways (2)

Introduction

On any reckoning this is a most important chapter as
the great figure of Elijah leaves the stage as suddenly and
dramatically as he had entered (1 Kings 17:1) and the as
yet little known figure of Elisha prepares to carry on the
work. Also it is a chapter full of incident and drama as well
as powerful teaching about the Word and work of Yahweh.
It is a story both of transition and continuity and has much
to say about such situations when a significant figure passes
on with their work done.

Plainly an important emphasis is to present Elisha as a
worthy successor to Elijah and to emphasise that Yahweh
is with him as much as He was with Elijah. It is not helpful
as some have done to see Elijah as a prophet of judgment
and Elisha as a prophet of grace. After all Elijah brought
the grace of God into the life and home of the widow of
Zarephath and Elisha brings judgment here in the incident
of the bears (2:23-25). There are perhaps differences of

style and situation (e.g. we learn in 5:9 that Elisha had a settled home) but the consistent theme, which as we have often seen is the overall theme of Kings, is that the Word of Yahweh spoken by His prophets known and unknown is powerful both in salvation and judgment.

Listening to the text

Context and structure

Chapter 2 follows from Elijah's last public confrontation with the house of Ahab as he brings Yahweh's judgment to Ahaziah (2 Kings 1) and is essentially, as we shall see, an authentication of his ministry. Also, as I shall suggest in the sermon outlines, it can usefully be preached along with 1 Kings 19:15-21 showing that Elisha has been involved with Elijah for some time which emphasises the continuity of the two prophetic ministries.

There are two clear parts (which will be subdivided in the next section)

+ Elijah finishes the race (2:1-12)

+ Elisha takes up the baton (2:13-25).

Working through the text

Elijah finishes the race (2:1-12)

This episode, one of the most powerful and dramatic in the Old Testament, is a journey which has two parts: a backward journey (vv. 1-10) and an upward journey (vv. 11-12). The inclusion of 'taking Elijah up to heaven' (v. 1) and 'Elijah went up to heaven' (v. 11) shows the unity of the story.

Looking first at the backward journey (vv. 1-10) it is important to emphasise that this is not a nostalgic wallowing in the past but a deliberate visiting of places where God's power had been shown in the past. More particularly there are echoes of the transition from Moses to Joshua. Just as Yahweh reassured Joshua 'as I was with Moses, so I will be with you' here Elisha is being given that same promise. Gilgal, Bethel and Jericho also appear to have been places where there were companies of prophets, but that is less important than the significance of the places themselves. Also it is important to notice that Elijah is determined to make sure that Elisha is committed to this journey as three times (vv. 2, 4, 6) he tells Elisha to stay and each time he insists on following.

They go to Gilgal, the place Israel set up base camp after crossing the Jordan (Josh. 4:21-24) and is a reminder of God's mighty acts as He brought Israel out of Egypt and into the promised land. See especially Joshua 4:23-24 which emphasise the power of Yahweh. Bethel goes back further to the story of the patriarchs for it was near there that Abraham built an altar and 'called on the name of Yahweh' (Gen. 12:8) and Jacob met God or more exactly God met Jacob (Gen. 28:10-22). Jericho was the place where Joshua met the commander of the Lord's armies (Josh. 5:13-15) and realised the battle was the Lord's. But the most powerful echo of God's mighty acts is when Elijah takes his cloak, the symbol of his prophetic office, as Moses had stretched his staff over the Red Sea. Once again the waters divide, showing that the God of Moses is the God of Elijah.

Elisha's request for 'a double portion of your spirit' is not saying he wants to be twice as good as Elijah but that he should receive the eldest son's share (Deut. 21:17). This son was responsible to carry on the family name and continue the father's work. Elijah's reply (v. 10) emphasises both the challenge and the privilege of carrying on the work. It is a challenge because of the demands and the sacrifices involved. Yet there is enormous privilege. 'See' (v. 10) does not simply mean be an eyewitness when the event happens but discern what the going of Elijah means about the essentially God-given nature of his ministry and the resources of heaven to carry it out. We are told in verse 15 that the company of the prophets 'watched' but failed to understand the inner meaning of what had happened.

Turning now to the upward journey (vv. 11-12) the first thing to notice is how suddenly heaven breaks into earth – 'as they were walking along and talking together' (v. 11). There is no attempt to explain the 'mechanics' of what happened anymore than in the case of Enoch (Gen. 5:24). But for Elijah the unseen world from which he had long drawn his strength and his message now becomes a visible reality. The whirlwind and fire are signs of God appearing: to Moses at the bush (Exod. 3:2) and at Sinai (Exod. 19:18); to Ezekiel (Ezek 1:4ff); to Job (Job 38:1; 40:6). The divine army is again to be significant in Elisha's story (2 Kings 6:8-23). There is poignancy in the phrase 'and Elisha saw him no more' as the realisation dawns that Elijah has gone and will not return. Everything seems suddenly defenceless. When Elisha speaks of 'the chariots and horsemen of Israel' he is probably not referring to the fiery chariots but to the way that Elijah and not Ahab's horses and chariots had been the true defence of Israel. He tears his own clothes and takes up Elijah's cloak as a sign that the mantle of Elijah is now his.

As we reflect on this incident two things stand out. The first is that this is God authenticating Elijah's ministry. I have already argued that writing off Elijah as spent force after 1 Kings 19 is imposing ideas on the text rather than listening to it. If there were any doubt this incident underlines that Elijah remained a powerful prophet to the very end. It is all too easy to see Elijah's ministry as a failure punctuated by a few dramatic episodes. After all he had failed to eliminate Baal worship; Ahab's house survived and idolatry was alive and well and the sinister Jezebel is still active until 2 Kings 9. However here God is honouring His servant by taking him straight to heaven and emphasising his continuity with Moses himself.

But more significantly this is a trailer for something much bigger. Our Lord's own ministry was by human standards a failure. Massive popularity and spectacular miracles soon gave way to hatred and rejection and to death on a cross. But God fully authenticated His ministry by raising Him from the dead and by His ascension, sending of the Spirit and the promise of His return in glorious majesty. When He returns all His people will be made like Him. Elijah's ministry is part of that great story and helps us to persevere.

Elisha carries on (2:13-25)
As Elisha begins his public ministry three episodes set the scene for what is to follow. The authenticating of Elisha as a true prophet (vv. 13-18); a miracle of mercy (vv. 19-22) and a judgment on mockers (vv. 23-25). These episodes show the character of the ministry which is to follow and which again show the twin themes of grace and judgment.

As Elisha steps out into prominence the episode of
the parting of the waters and the unsuccessful search by
the company of the prophets (vv. 13-18) authenticate his
ministry both positively and negatively. First the parting
of the waters (vv. 13-14) shows he has indeed inherited a
double portion of Elijah's spirit. The waters were parted
both for Moses and Elijah and this shows that Elisha is
a true prophet in their succession. This is not magic but a
symbolic action showing the power of the Creator to work
in His creation and to remove barriers as He pleases. It is
not the mantle but the living God who parts the waters. In
a much later generation the Prophet Zechariah is to make a
similar emphasis – 'not by might , nor by power, but by my
Spirit says Yahweh of hosts'. This is confirmed by Elisha's
question, not 'where is Elijah?' but 'where is Yahweh the
God of Elijah?'

This positive authentication of Elisha is confirmed
negatively as we see by contrast with the company of the
prophets whose concern is not with Yahweh but with
finding Elijah as they go on a futile three-day search for
him against Elisha's wishes (vv. 15-18). Elisha reluctantly
lets them go because they have to be made to realise how
pointless the search is. They are still stuck in the past , more
concerned about Elijah than about Elijah's God.

The next episode (vv. 19-21) is a miracle of mercy and, as
with Elijah, especially in 1 Kings 17, this is for the blessing of
others and not the aggrandisement of the prophet. Jericho
was under the curse of God (Josh. 6:26) and that curse had
been experienced by the man who rebuilt the city in the
time of Ahab (1 Kings 16:34). I suggested in the exposition
of that chapter (in the previous volume) that the implication
is that he rebuilt the city with Ahab's connivance. Yet

Jericho was also a place that had experienced grace as in the story of Rahab (Josh. 2:1-21;6:25) and it was to experience grace again. The method Elisha used is probably symbolic: the new bowl symbolising clean-ness and the salt as a preservative. But again the mechanics of the miracle is not what the incident is about. It was Yahweh who healed the water and He did it to confirm the Word spoken by Elisha. The emphasis is on the power of the Word. Here is a true picture of Gospel grace coming into death and leading to life.

The final incident (vv. 23-25) is by contrast a Word of judgment. Bethel, as already noted, was where Abraham first built an altar (Gen. 12:8) and Jacob met God (Gen. 28:10-21) but more recently had been made a centre of idolatry by Jeroboam, son of Nebat (1 Kings 12:29-33). This story has been condemned for its barbarity and as an excessive over-reaction to a trivial insult but that is a hasty and superficial reaction. First Elisha is not looking for trouble; the 'youths' come out probably in search of some diversion. The second is the word translated 'youths' (NIV), 'little children' (KJV), 'small boy' (ESV). The word is na'ar which like the English word 'boy' or 'lad' can reflect a wide range of meanings such as 'our boy' could be a man. Jeremiah calls himself a na'ar (Jer. 1:6) but plainly he must at least be in his teens. The shade of meaning has to be determined by the context. Here the bears maul forty-two of the youths which suggests that there must be a large body of them. This is far more likely to be youths or young men than small boys; in other words a very threatening group. I think we must imagine a gang of young men looking for trouble and prepared to pick a fight.

We must further look at what they said. 'Baldie' may not be a pleasant jibe but that is not the point. 'Go up' is an irreverent reference to Elijah's ascension and basically mockery of both prophets. This is probably a reflection of the idolatrous attitudes of Bethel and shows this is more sinister than a tasteless jibe.

But the whole point is that this is a judgment of Yahweh, not a petulant prophet over-reaching himself. When Elisha calls down a curse in the name of Yahweh and Yahweh responds, this is a sign that God is judging. In Acts 19:13 the seven sons of the high priest command demons to come out 'in the name of Jesus whom Paul preaches'. The evil spirit does indeed come out but turns on them realising they are no true representatives of the Lord Christ. Here by contrast Yahweh again authenticates Elisha, this time in judgment.

So this section shows that Elisha is God's man just as Elijah had been, and that Elisha is the instrument of God's Word both in blessing and judgment. The chapter concludes with Elisha returning to Mt Carmel, the place where Yahweh had revealed Himself as the true God (1 Kings 18) and then to Samaria where the prophetic testimony to the house of Ahab is to continue.

From text to message

Getting the message clear: the theme
God does not leave Himself without a witness and, as the powerful ministry of Elijah draws to a close, He already has His man in place to follow and indeed develop that ministry into its next phase. The powerful Word of God both in salvation and judgment is central.

Getting the message clear: the aim
The most important lesson of this chapter is that the Word
of God continues to have power throughout the generations.
Leaders and preachers come and go but the Word of God
remains living and relevant in each new generation. It is
effective both in blessing and judgment.

A way in
One way of introducing the passage would be to talk about
the death of Winston Churchill in January 1965. People
who were old or middle aged at that time spoke of the end
of an era and although the Second World War had ended
nearly twenty years before some felt that the nation was
now vulnerable with the passing of the great war leader.
Just as here (v. 12) Elisha sees Elijah as the true defender
of the nation. That analogy like all others is limited but it
might be helpful.

On a more communal or personal level most of us have
experienced such times. An influential church leader moves
on, perhaps retires or dies and there is the inevitable sense
of bereavement and an uncertainty about the future. In our
personal lives the death of grandparents and parents leaves
a void.

Ideas for application

+   We need to emphasise that when leaders pass on, while
     we will inevitably miss them we must not wallow in
     nostalgia and pine for a return to 'the good old days'.
     John Wesley said 'God buries His workers and carries
     on His work'. We must remember that we have the
     same God and the same Bible and 'everything we need
     for life and godliness' (2 Pet. 1:3). Remember as well

the words of Jacob to Joseph 'I am about to die but God will be with you' (Gen. 48:21).

+ This will be an antidote to the celebrity culture which has gripped evangelicalism. This is shown here by the company of the prophets whose main concern is to find Elijah. Rather, like Elisha, we need to look to the Lord who will carry on His work.

+ At the same time we must avoid the opposite extreme of denigrating leaders. Hebrews 13:7 says, 'Remember your leaders who spoke the Word of God to you'. Here is the correct balance; it is important to recognise those who speak the Word of God and who are reliable and sometimes inspirational speakers of that Word. This is part of honouring the God of the Word.

+ There is the question of how committed we are to following the Lord, shown by Elisha's threefold insistence that he is staying with Elijah to the end. The importance of perseverance in the life of faith needs to be emphasised.

+ We need to preach the whole message, judgment as well as salvation, and not be afraid to do this. There are negatives which bring out the positives.

+ The ascension of Elijah to heaven and the falling of his mantle on Elisha points us to the ascended Lord who sent the Spirit and gave gifts to carry on the work (Eph. 4:7-12).

Suggestions for preaching

The chapter could be preached as a whole or divided into two and here are some examples of how this might be done.

Sermon 1
This would take the chapter as a whole with some such title as 'Where now is the Lord?'

Introduction
Transition as God takes one servant to heaven and has His man ready for the next stage

The Journey taken (2:1-10)

+ Significance of places visited – see exposition.

+ The showing of Elisha's commitment.

The Destination reached (2:11-12)

+ The mystery of the ascension – pointing to Christ's own.

+ The authentication of Elijah's ministry.

The work goes on (2:13-25)

+ Elisha is an authentic successor – spirit not ultimately Elijah's but Spirit of God.

+ God is always bringing on new people.

+ Gospel of salvation and judgment continues.

Sermon 2
This would focus on (with a slightly different chapter division – 2:1-14) Elijah's going and might use some such title as 'Elijah finishes the race'.

Introduction
This is a work of God as emphasised by the mention of the Lord's activity (vv. 1 and 14). Focus on the theme of journey.

Backward Journey (vv. 1-10) – making similar points as in sermon 1

Upward Journey (vv. 11-12a) – again as in sermon 1 emphasising how it points to Christ's ascension

Onward Journey (vv. 12b-14) – God not limited to certain people and places

Sermon 3

If you were preaching a series on Elijah and Elisha then it might be useful to look back at 1 Kings 19:15-21 and pick up the story of Elisha's original call. The sermon would then focus on 2 Kings 2:13-25. A title like ' The living Word remains powerful' would show the emphasis of the sermon.

Introduction

The Word which came through Elijah will continue in Elisha's ministry and this sets the tone for both men's work.

The Word is more powerful than kings and nations (1 Kings 19:15-21)

+ The Word will depose and set up kings (see 2 Kings 8–9).

+ The prophet's authority is greater than the power of kings.

The Word comes in the power of the Spirit (2:13-18)
Similar to points made about this passage in sermon 1.

The Word brings both salvation and judgment (2:19-25)

+ Life in place of curse (vv. 19-22).

+ Death because of rebellion (vv. 23-25).

Suggestions for teaching

Questions to help understand the passage

1. What is the significance of the places which Elijah and Elisha visit?

2. Why does Elijah seem to discourage Elisha from going with him? (vv. 1, 4, 6)

3. Why does Elisha ask for a double portion of Elijah's spirit? (v. 9)

4. What does the whirlwind suggest about what is happening?

5. Why does Elisha strike the water with Elijah's mantle?

6. Why do the company of the prophets insist on searching for Elijah? (vv. 15-18)

7. How do we know the healing of the water (vv. 19-22) is not magic?

8. What suggests the 'youths' (vv. 23-25) are not harmless children?

9. Why does Elisha go to Mount Carmel?

Questions to help apply the passage

1. In what way does Elijah point to Christ in this passage? You might like to read Acts 1:6-11.

2. What is the spiritual significance of the places visited in vv. 1-6 and how does this show that this is not simply a nostalgic journey?

3. How does verse 12 show the overwhelming significance of Elijah in national life and how does this give us a sense of perspective on the church in the world?

4. How does Elisha's question in verse 14 show us the way to think and act when leaders move on?

5. How does the attitude of the company of the prophets (vv. 15-18) warn us that we do not rely on men however important they may be?

6. How can we teach the gospel of grace from the little incident of the healing of the water? (vv. 19-22)

7. What does the incident in verses 23-25 tell us about judgment?

3

THE WORD WHICH OVERTHROWS
KINGDOMS (3)

Introduction

Elisha's ministry is now to be the dominant theme until chapter 8 and he will not leave the stage completely until chapter 13. This episode reminds us of his commissioning in 1 Kings 19:15-17 where Yahweh had shown to Elijah that the prophetic Word establishes and tears down kings and kingdoms. There are further clear echoes of 1 Kings 22 particularly in the role played by Jehoshaphat. We have often seen throughout 1 Kings the enduring power of the Word of God and that emphasis is to be at the heart of 2 Kings.

Just a word on history for the sharp eyed reader. Jehoram here, son of Ahab, has the same name as his Judaean contemporary whose reign is briefly described in 2 Kings 8:16-24. The name is also spelled Joram. The problem is that 1:17b says that northern Jehoram became king in the second year of southern Jehoram but 3:1 says he became king in the eighteenth year of Jehoshaphat.

The problem is resolved if we see (as 8:16 says) that he was co-regent with his father Jehoshaphat. Here the dating draws attention to the fact that Jehoshaphat was still on the throne and continuing his unhelpful alliance with the house of Ahab as in 1 Kings 22.

So we are dealing with history but more importantly the shaping of that history by the Word of God through His prophets. This theme is underlined in the New Testament as well. Two examples will suffice. In Luke 3:1-2 there is a roll call of the powerful from emperor to high priest but all are bypassed as the Word of God comes to John the Baptist. In 2 Corinthians 10:4 Paul writes, 'The weapons of our warfare are not of the flesh but have divine power to destroy strongholds'. So here the author of Kings never tires in showing us the power of God's Word to destroy strongholds and thus encourage us to have confidence in it.

Listening to the text

Context and structure

This is to be the first public appearance of Elisha after he has inherited Elijah's mantle. He is now to be centre stage until chapter 8 and is to be involved both in political dramas and in ministry to unknown people.

The narrative develops in 4 acts:

+ Jehoram found wanting (3:1-3)

+ An uneasy alliance (3:4-12)

+ A prophetic drama (3:13-20)

+ A grim judgment (3:21-27)

Working through the text

Jehoram found wanting (3:1-3)

At first sight it may appear as if the situation in the northern kingdom has improved, for Jehoram is not as blatant a sinner as Ahab and Jezebel and he removed 'the pillar of Baal' which was a sacred stone. In other words, he got rid of the more blatant signs of Baalism. However it is always easier to remove idols from the public spaces than to remove idols from hearts.

This is surely the point of verse 3. Jehoram 'clung' to the sins of Jeroboam. This is the word used in Genesis 2:24 of a man holding fast to his wife. Jeroboam's religious policies are outlined in 1 Kings 12:25-33 and his trendy syncretism may have looked less offensive than the undiluted paganism of Ahab but it comes under the same condemnation because it dethrones Yahweh and despises His Word. It may be less blatant but ultimately it comes under God's judgment.

An uneasy alliance (3:4-12)

The rebellion of Moab has already been mentioned in 2 Kings 1:1 and Jehoram, like his father before him, calls on the help of Jehoshaphat. The king of Edom (v. 9) was probably a vassal of Judah (cf. 1 Kings 22:47). They journey south to avoid the strongly fortified places in northern Moab but as they skirt the Dead Sea they encounter desert and run out of water. It is difficult to avoid recalling the great drought of 1 Kings 17, 18 which was Yahweh's judgment and also to remember that only Yahweh can provide water as in the Exodus story (eg. Exod. 17:1-7; Num. 20:1-13).

Jehoram reacts to this by blaming Yahweh (v. 10) combining the language of piety and grumbling. 'The LORD has called these three kings' recalls Genesis 3:12 – 'the

woman whom you gave to be with me'. Blame the Lord for
the mess you have created and then expect Him to get you
out of it; that is surely true of our human nature.

Jehoshaphat is a very different kind of man from Jehoram.
For one thing he is a true believer and again asks Jehoram
the question he had asked his father (1 Kings 22:7). As we
have seen, the king of Judah genuinely wants to hear from
Yahweh but he has an almost congenital need to snuggle
up to the house of Ahab. That is a perpetual danger,
failing to see who God's enemies are and ending in unwise
compromises. In 1 Kings 22 it had almost cost Jehoshaphat
his life. Yet here Jehoshaphat again looks for a Word from
Yahweh while Jehoram panics.

A prophetic drama (3:13-20)
We are not told why Elisha was there but ultimately, as
with Elijah, it is the providence of God which puts him
where he can be most useful. Like Elijah with Ahab, Elisha
does not waste time in small talk with Jehoram. He does
not commend the king of Israel for not being as bad as his
father rather he exposes Jehoram's insincerity. Jehoram had
not asked Yahweh's guidance before this military adventure
and now simply wants to get out of a tight corner rather
than genuinely hearing a prophetic Word. After all, if the
pagan gods are true gods why can they not help?

Elisha's respectful treatment of Jehoshaphat is double-
edged. Partly it is a reminder to the king of Judah who
his true friends are and the dubious company he is
presently keeping. Yet there is grace here as well. For all
his weaknesses, Jehoshaphat was the Davidic king to whom
God's promises had been made and in his reign there were
genuine glimpses of the King who was to come. Since Christ

is Prophet as well as King, Elisha here as he provides water and promises victory also points to the true fulfilment of what is partially seen here.

The spoken Word is to be accompanied by a visible sign. The first part is Elisha calling for a musician. This is not to be regarded as an irrelevant detail because there are other examples of this: notably David playing the harp to expel the evil spirit from Saul (1 Sam. 16:23). As the harpist plays, Elisha prophesies that God will not only provide water which is 'an easy thing' but will hand over Moab as well. Here is a reminder not to limit the God who 'is able to do immeasurably more than we can ask or imagine' (Eph. 3:20).

There are definite echoes here of Elijah on Carmel where in 1 Kings 18:32 he commands a trench to be built and filled with water. The same principle is operating: we can build trenches or ditches but only God can send water. Another important point which controls this section is verse 14 and the reference to Jehoshaphat already noticed. The king of Israel and, for that matter, the king of Edom are safe only because the Davidic king is with them. Jehoram had no reason to expect a miracle from Yahweh whom he had failed to honour. However, Jehoshaphat's presence was a sign of grace and a call to Jehoram to turn to Yahweh. If Jehoram was (as is probable) the unnamed 'king of Israel' in chapter 5 where Naaman is healed and in chapter 8 where the siege of Samaria is lifted, then he was to have further such opportunities. Today the Greater Son not just of Jehoshaphat but of David is our only guarantee of the salvation and blessing of God.

A grim judgment (3:21-27)

The Moabites misunderstand the flowing water lit by the morning sun as blood and assume the coalition has self-destructed but instead are destroyed themselves. Kir Harasheth, Moab's principal southern city, survives and becomes the scene of a human sacrifice. The king of Moab takes two actions: first is to break through the surrounding forces but that fails; second is to offer his son as a human sacrifice to Chemosh, Moab's national god. This second action succeeds and we need to ask what exactly is behind verse 27?

There are two issues here, the first being human sacrifice which shows not only panic and cruelty on the part of the king of Moab but also the nastiness of pagan gods. The author is showing both the futility and darkness of paganism. But again we see how pagan gods are without grace and without any light to guide us. We are again reminded of the futile and frantic ravings of Baal's prophets on Mt Carmel (1 Kings 18:27-29).

The other and somewhat puzzling phrase is 'great anger was upon Israel'. The problem is whose anger is it and why does it come on Israel? Some have argued that the anger was that of the Moabite god Chemosh, furious at Israel for invading his land. But that view is untenable. Chemosh could no more show military muscle than Baal could send fire or rain (1 Kings 18). Our author will not concede any power at all to a pagan godlet. Others have argued that the anger is of the Moabites themselves who turn on Israel and drive them out of their land. But the Word translated 'against' could also be 'upon', ie. furious anger came on Israel because of the sacrifice of the king's son. If this is the case it could be yet another Word to Jehoram to remember the love and mercy of Yahweh in contrast to the barbarities of paganism. In any case the victory over Moab would have left an unpleasant taste in their mouths and they would have returned home with little satisfaction.

From text to message

Getting the message clear: the theme
The theme is the underlying one of the whole book which is how the prophetic Word is more powerful than kings and kingdoms. More specifically here it is about prophetic authority represented by Elisha. Already in chapter 2 he had inherited Elijah's mantle and shown both the mercy of God in the healing of the water and the judgment of God in the incident of the bears. Now he intervenes in the affairs of state as Elijah had done with Ahab and Ahaziah.

Getting the message clear: the aim
The Word of God gives clear guidance and provides safety when human plans fail, as here the water dries up in the desert of Edom. There is the further contrast between the mercy of Yahweh and the grisly rites demanded by Chemosh the Moabite god.

A way in
We might approach this similar to the way we often tend to rush into projects without prayer. No one prays here for Yahweh's guidance before setting out for Moab. Only belatedly is Elisha asked for a Word from Yahweh. Bible reading and prayer need to be the driving force of all our activities, not just our Sunday services.

Ideas for application

+ Idolatry is still idolatry even if it shows itself in a less crude way. It is still something which takes over people's lives. Jehoram 'clung to' idols and made the deliberate decision 'not to turn away' (v. 3). The Lord will not share with idols.

+ There is a warning over compromising alliances (v. 7). As we have seen Jehoshaphat is a good man but he cannot bring himself to say 'no'. This kind of association may be politically expedient but will lead to danger and further compromise.

+ There is always a need to bring the Word of God to bear in every situation. When that Word comes it is crisp and decisive. Not least that it cuts through pretence and humbug as it does here (v. 13). We need to beware of those like Jehoram who reject the Lord and then use pious language to cover up their insincerity.

+ We cannot bring water but we can dig ditches. That is, we cannot convert people or cause them to grow in grace but we can bring the Word to them.

+ Paganism and syncretism for all their apparent liberalism are in fact cruel and intolerant. The action of the king of Moab in trying to appease his god shows that Chemosh was conceived of as bitter and revengeful and bloodthirsty. There is no grace in such a religion.

Suggestions for preaching

Sermon 1

A title such as 'The disturbing Word' would place the focus on the prophetic message. A brief historical note about the Jehorams of Israel and Judah would be helpful. This should not be overdone but a brief reminder that the author is concerned about historical accuracy. Then focus on the power of the Word of God in the world of politics.

Not treating the Word seriously (3:1-12)

+ Pick and mix approach of Jehoram.

+ The compromised approach of Jehoshaphat.

Unleashing the Word of God (vv. 3:13-25)

+ The way it cuts through pretence (3:13, 14).

+ The way it does more than we can imagine (vv. 18, 19).

Results of ignoring the Word of God (3:26, 27).

+ The grimness of paganism.

+ The unsatisfactory victory.

Sermon 2

This would still emphasise the Word but focus on the reactions of the characters under a title such as 'Kings, Prophets and the Word'. Again the introduction would briefly outline the historical situation.

Jehoram plays with the Word

+ Semi-paganism is still idolatry.

+ Pious language is no substitute for living faith.

Jehoshaphat wants to hear the Word

+ Compromised but still open.

+ Knows where the genuine Word will be found.

+ Is respected as the Davidic king.

Elisha fearlessly proclaims the Word

+ Points out failure of unbelieving prophets.

+ Shows power of the Word.

+ Not censorious and shows respect for Jehoshaphat king of Judah.

A kind of footnote would be to point out how different was the 'Word' of the god of Moab.

Suggestions for teaching

Questions to help understand the passage

1. What is the point of the brief account of Jehoram's reign in verses 1-3? Does this help us to understand what is to follow?

2. What does verse 7 tell us about Jehoshaphat? You might like to refer back to 1 Kings 22:4.

3. Why do you think Jehoram claims that Yahweh has sent them on this expedition?

4. What further aspect of Jehoshaphat's character is revealed in verse 11? Again you might like to look at 1 Kings 22:5, 7.

5. Why is Elisha so abrupt with Jehoram?

6. What is the significance of the musician?

7. Why do you think the Moabites assumed the sunlight on the water was blood? Does this suggest that God might have prevented them seeing reality?

8. What does 'fury against Israel' mean? (v. 27)

Questions to help apply the passage

1. Jehoram was not as evil as his father and mother (vv. 1-2). How does the author show that what he did was no less fatal and how do we guard against this kind of semi- paganism which can infiltrate our lives and churches so easily?

2. Jehoshaphat was basically a good man but seemed unable to avoid alliances with the house of Ahab. What form might such compromise take today?

3. Jehoram uses pious language to hide his real feelings. In what circumstances might we be tempted to do this? What are some of the situations we see this approach adopted by others?

4. Jehoshaphat was flawed but faithful. How do we ensure the true voice of God is heard?

5. Elisha's words about Jehoshaphat remind us that our safety is because of our relationship with the true Davidic king. How do we keep that in the forefront of our living and preaching?

6. Verse 18 shows us that God can do immeasurably more than we can ask or think. How do we limit God in our thinking and praying?

7. How does verse 27 help us to expose the lies of paganism and how do we show that worldviews

which do not have grace at their heart are ultimately cruel and inhumane?

8. How do we know that this victory left a sour taste and what do we learn about the gulf between the Lord and false gods?

4

The Life-Giving Word (4)

Introduction

We are now well into Elisha's story and here a cluster of incidents with him at the heart demonstrate both the power of God's life-giving Word and the vulnerability of humans. It is a rich chapter and the temptation is to focus on the long central episode of the raising of the dead boy and skim over the other incidents. It is certainly possible to take that central incident as a sermon on its own and we shall look at different ways of preaching the chapter, but there is also much to learn in the shorter stories which supplement the message of the raising of the boy.

An important aspect of all the stories in this chapter is that we are away from the world of power politics. Elisha certainly has been involved in the world of kings and armies and he will be again but here it is the normal business of life in which the Word which causes the rise and fall of kingdoms operates. The chapter shows that all of life belongs to God and nothing, including death, is outside His control.

One of the values of a chapter like this is the contrast between extended narrative and brief notes. All life and every individual matters to Yahweh. Sometimes we are given extended coverage of a particular incident because it particularly draws attention to certain aspects of His grace and power and other times there are brief glimpses reminding us of how He operates in the hidden and unseen with unknown people.

Listening to the text

Context and structure
Elisha's status as true prophet and successor to Elijah has already been established (chapter 2) and his importance on the national stage underlined (chapter 3). Now he is shown moving among the people who have no particular role in national politics and thus his role as a truly national prophet is established.

The text falls naturally into four parts which are the four stories.

+   God's generosity helps the helpless (4:1-7)

+   God's power raises the dead (4:8-37)

+   God's grace overrules mistakes (4:38-41)

+   God's generosity gives more than is needed (4:42-44)

Working through the text

God's generosity helps the helpless (4:1-7)
The situation here is desperate: death followed by debt. It is possible that the prophet had been killed as a result of state

persecution. In any case, his widow is destitute and likely to be made more so by the removal of her sons. So often this kind of thing happens: a faithful young man dies of cancer, leaving a young widow and small children; a man of integrity is ruined by corrupt business associates; a woman spends the best years of her life caring for elderly parents and, when they die, is left alone and without a home. 'Revering the LORD' is no immunity badge from disaster.

Yet in this widow's desperation there is faith and, recognising the true prophet, she cries out for help. She tells Elisha the problem and does not try to suggest solutions. There is an interesting contrast with Jehoram (3:13,14) who is dismissed by Elisha as a God-dishonourer and charlatan. Here the prophet is only interested in helping the widow and treating her with the compassion of the God he serves.

God begins with what she has, 'what do you have in your house?' What she has, a little oil, is a sign of destitution and helplessness. Elisha does not intrude; indeed once he asks the woman to collect the jars from her neighbours, he is in the background and the power of God is at work. And it is at work secretly, behind closed doors and the supply of oil was only limited by the supply of empty vessels but more than enough was given.

Then Elisha tells her what to do: pay off the debt, save your sons from slavery and there is more than enough to live on. God is never niggardly giving only basic necessity. Surely we look forward to the Lake of Galilee where not only is the crowd's basic hunger satisfied but twelve baskets are filled with the remains of the feast (Matt. 14:13-21; Mark 6:32-44; Luke 9:10-17; John 6:1-13). This God is our God, and He is the God who gives leftovers.

God's power raises the dead (4:8-37)

This is by far the longest of the four stories and combines real joy and real sorrow and is above all about grace which throws open a window into God's heart. Once again Elisha is the channel of that grace as he so often is to the believing remnant. The narrative develops in three movements.

The first scene (4:8-17) shows God's grace responding to need. Shunem is south of the Sea of Galilee and on a regularly travelled route. The woman is unnamed but in very comfortable circumstances. We are not told how she knew that Elisha was 'a holy man of God' but it is clearly an example of spiritual perception and an indication that faith had not totally died out in Jehoram's Israel. That is first shown by her practical and generous hospitality as she prepares a guest room for Elisha (v.10).

This is matched by Elisha's warm and grateful response and his desire to repay her generosity. Thus he learns of her secret sorrow; comfortable and wealthy as she is, she longs for a son, which with an old husband seems remote. Elisha promises she will have a son and, not surprisingly the woman finds this hard to believe. What is happening? We have a clue in verse 16 ' about this time next year' which is the phrase used in Genesis 18:10 of the promise to Sarah. This occurs elsewhere: Rebekah has to wait twenty years for a child (Gen. 25:19-26); Rachel the favourite waiting for Joseph (Gen. 29:31-30:24); Manoah's wife waiting for a child (Judges 13:2); Hannah waiting for Samuel (1 Sam. 1:10-11); Elizabeth (Luke 1:7).

Yet there is a big difference here. In these other cases the birth was necessary to carry on the line of promise or to bring a great leader for a time of crisis. Here it is pure grace. We know nothing about the future of this boy; God loved this woman and wanted to make her happy. We need to be less restrictive in our ideas of God and His amazing, overflowing grace

The second scene (4:18-26) is about puzzling grace. For a short time all is life and joy : 'gave birth' (v. 17) and 'grew' (v. 18). Then tragedy strikes and the wealthy woman loses her son, contrasting with the poor woman earlier in the chapter who had managed to keep hers. The wealthy woman hurries to Mount Carmel, more than fifteen miles away and leaves the child on Elisha's bed. She does not know if he can help but she knows he is a man of God and thus in touch with the only One who can.

We also see that her husband does not share her faith. His world-view is captured succinctly in verse 23. Men of God are for special days and irrelevant in the real business of living. A God who is only for Sundays and special occasions will soon become boring.

The third scene (4:27-37) is about grace which defies death. As in all episodes of raising the dead there is mystery and we need humility in the face of such unanswered questions. This is not a story of magic ritual, still less is it an example of the 'kiss of life', this is the Lord of life storming the kingdom of death and anticipating the time when that last enemy will be destroyed.

A clear distinction between Elisha and Gehazi emerges clearly in verses 29-31. Elisha told Gehazi to lay his staff on the boy's body as a sign it was not to be moved. Gehazi misinterprets that to mean that the staff is magical and will bring the boy back to life. It is always easy to trust in techniques but they do not bring life.

Notice Elisha's dependence on Yahweh. He 'prayed to the LORD' (v. 33). This shows that any action he took was

not magical. The boy is restored to life and to his mother.
We hear no more of either of them because the main point
of the story is that the God of Israel can raise the dead.
It was just a few miles from Shunem in the town of Nain
that Jesus raised another son from the dead (Luke 7:11-17).
Both these miracles pointed to the kingdom of God, to the
new creation where death is no longer.

This God scatters good gifts throughout our earthly
lives but as long as we are in this world, joy will be mixed
with sorrow and triumph with tragedy. Yet what these
stories show us is that God's generosity is magnificent and
that His grace knows no limits. Not even death can stop
the coming of His kingdom.

God's grace overrules mistakes (4:38-41)
Some see this story as trivial but that is to ignore the
importance of eating to all communities. The verb 'to
eat' dominates both this story and the next. Eating is
an important sub-theme throughout the Bible from the
catastrophic eating in Eden to the 'take eat' of the Gospel.
When we add to that the metaphor of the new creation
as a feast as well as the significance of eating together we
see that this apparently trivial incident leads us right to the
heart of the Gospel.

This is a visible sign of God at work. Back in chapter
2:19-21 Elisha had used salt to cleanse polluted water, here
it is flour to cleanse poisoned food. This is not magic but
a visible sign of God's grace. Much of the time we have to
trust and obey God's Word without such signs. But there
are times when God in His grace gives visible and tangible
evidence of His power with the object of strengthening
faith, and here further authenticating His prophet. Indeed,

this in its small way points to the removal of the curse and the restored creation.

On the human level this is the story of a mistake, not of a crime. The man who put the herbs in the pot was not malicious, indeed he was trying to supplement their meal at a time of famine. This is our experience so often; well-meaning attempts to 'help' result in chaos. God graciously overrules and all is well.

God's generosity gives more than is needed (4:42-44)

The final episode also comes from the time of famine and also relates to eating. The first thing to notice is that there are still some faithful people around. This unnamed man from Baal Shalisha, somewhere in the hill country of Ephraim, brought newly baked bread to Elisha. Deuteronomy 18:4-5 specified such first fruits were to be given to the priest. However, many of these still served Baal and others doubtless followed Jehoram's pick and mix religion. This man was one of the believing remnant who knew where true spiritual authority was.

This time there is no visible sign, only the simple Word of God through the prophet and both the initial feeding and the left overs are 'according to the Word of the LORD' (v. 44). This echoes the faithful provision of God for His people in the desert (Deut. 8:2-3), the passage that links physical eating with the life-giving power of God's Word.

All this points forward to one greater than Elisha. The chapter ends as it began with a miracle of provision for need. We have already noticed the links with the feeding of the five thousand told in all four Gospels. Even more than here, these stories of Jesus' miraculous provision of far more than is necessary is a sign of our total inadequacy and

complete dependence on Him. These stories here as well
are about a good and generous God who does not need us
but graciously takes us and our little gifts and transforms
them.

From text to message

Getting the message clear: the theme
This group of stories shows the life-giving power of God's
Word in a series of hopeless circumstances: poverty, debt,
famine and death itself. God is not limited by us and our
lack of resources. His Word is the agent in all the life-
bringing events in the chapter and that needs to be a major
emphasis.

Getting the message clear: the aim
To give us renewed confidence in the power of God to
tackle humanly impossible situations. Also to show the
loving and generous way in which this power is exercised
and how the Lord cares for the weak and helpless and the
vulnerable. Also to give confidence in the life-giving power
of the Word of God in our world.

A way in
I know we have to be careful of stories of revival and many
spend their lives longing for the sensational. However, we
must not fall into the opposite extreme and think God
can never work in unusual ways. We might talk about the
deadness of the church throughout this country in the late
eighteenth century and the sense of hopelessness that the
work of God would ever flourish again. Then God laid
His hand on the Wesleys and Whitefield and within a few
short years revival was a reality. This is not a call to say that

because God worked then He must work now but rather an encouraging reminder that we can never limit Him or know when He will choose to work.

Ideas for application

+ The chapter shows us God's concern for ordinary people. The only named person is Elisha himself and his total dependence on the Lord is emphasised. This is a lesson we need to learn in our day of celebrity culture and big names. Too often the glory is given to the servant rather than the Lord and name-dropping and cultivating the famous rather than thanking God for His gifts is a feature of our evangelical life.

+ An important emphasis is human vulnerability. This is not just in the case of the destitute widow but with the well-to-do woman of Shunem when her son dies. Richard Baxter's words are appropriate here: 'I preach as never sure to preach again, and as a dying man to dying men'.

+ The important truth that God overrules our mistakes is particularly clear in the story of the poisoned stew (38-41). This would make us less concerned always to justify ourselves. We are fallible as well as vulnerable and a frank admission of error would often defuse tense situations.

+ God's interest in everyday things lies at the heart of the chapter. He cares about eating, about a place for His servant to rest. He cares about our homes and families, about babysitting, about paying the bills, about work and holidays. We must not be super-spiritual.

✦   Above all this is a great chapter to preach Christ from. It points to the early days of Jesus' ministry, continual miracles and the challenging of disease, sin and death, a ministry amongst normal, unnamed people where His Word was powerful and His compassion was seen. But they also point forward to His reign in the new creation when all these dark powers will be banished for ever.

Suggestions for preaching

This is a long and rich chapter and could be preached in different ways. A sermon on the whole chapter would have to be careful not to cram too much in and realise that it could not focus on every detail.

Sermon 1

The emphasis here would be on God's overwhelming generosity. This could be done by taking the four sections of the chapter outlined above and developing the sermon in the way suggested by the section on 'Listening to the text'. The problem there would be that the section on the woman of Shunem is so much longer than the others that the shape of the sermon could be skewed. It would probably therefore be better to take a more thematic approach.

• *The amazing generosity of God:* in the widow episode (4:1-8) and the new bread (4:42-44) He not only satisfies the immediate need but there is much left over.

• *The power of God against things we fear:* debt; poverty; death itself.

- *The life-giving power of the Word of God* – Elisha is the faithful servant who is the channel of God's power and this is shown by his prayerful dependence.

This sermon would use the detail of the different stories to illustrate the different points and would be God-centred.

Sermon 2

This would take the three shorter stories and preach them as a separate sermon; treating the longer story in a sermon on its own. The stories are probably not chronological but thematically grouped (as often in the Elisha stories) so nothing would be lost.

- *God's generosity to the helpless* (4:1-7) – This is a tragedy in Elijah's own circle 'the company of the prophets' – human helplessness meets God's power; human need meets God's provision – when we were helpless Christ died for us.

- *God's generosity in our mistakes* (4:38-41) – say something about eating and its significance as suggested in the exposition – well-meaning mistakes can be used by God for His glory.

- *God's generosity giving far more than we need* (4:42-44) – faithful remnant and inadequate resources which God multiplied – bring in Feeding of 5,000 and point to Christ the Bread of Heaven both for the journey and fully in the new creation.

Sermon 3

This would focus on the woman of Shunem (4:8-37) and the life-giving Word facing its biggest challenge, death itself, again a story drenched in grace.

- *Grace which responds to need* (4:8-17) – a woman of spiritual perception and a grateful prophet – He sees her real need and brings help – this child is not in the line of promise – God wants to give.

- *Grace which puzzles* (4:18-26) – Why does the Lord give and snatch away? Human tragedy but faith of woman as opposed to her insensitive husband. She realises the only help is in the God of Elisha.

- *Grace which defies death* (4:27-37) – not magic but life-giving power of God. Go beyond this story to the raising of the widow's son in Luke 7 anticipating the day when all the dead will hear the voice of the Son of God (John 5:28,29).

Suggestions for teaching

Questions to help understand the passage

1. How does the writer show how totally destitute the widow was? (vv. 1-3)

2. How do we know this woman had faith? (See vv. 1 and 5.)

3. How do we know the woman of Shunem was exceptionally generous? (vv. 8-10)

4. How do we know Elisha does not take this hospitality for granted? (vv. 11-13)

5. How does the author convey the almost unbearable poignancy of the boy's death? (vv. 17-20)

6. What do we learn about the different attitudes of the woman and her husband? (vv. 22, 23)

7. Gehazi comes out in a bad light. How does the author show this? (vv. 27-31)

8. Why is what Elisha does in verse 33 more important than what he does in verses 34-35?

9. What does the incident of the poisoned stew (vv. 38-41) show about the extent of God's interests?

10. How do we know the man from Baal Shalisha (vv. 42-44) is part of the faithful remnant? Have a look at Deuteronomy 18:4-5.

Questions to help apply the passage

1. The widow (v. 5) obeys Elisha and does it without fuss. Are we too ready to make public what we see as our achievements rather than give God glory?

2. How does the woman of Shunem show spiritual perception? What can we learn about the fact that she describes Elisha as 'a holy man of God' rather than talk about his exploits?

3. We tend to imagine that people of wealth and standing are not as vulnerable as others. How does the woman's sadness help us in being sensitive to others?

4. Many long to have children but can't and some have lost children. How would we treat a passage like this in a sensitive way knowing that there will probably be such people present?

5. The husband clearly thinks men of God are for 'religious' occasions? How do we avoid a 'Sunday' faith?

6. Gehazi believes in the magic properties of Elisha's staff. How do we avoid being too reliant on methods and techniques?

7. How does Elisha show his total dependence on God? Have we anything to learn from the fact he closed the door (v. 33)? It would be useful to look at Matthew 6:5-8.

8. God overruled the man's well-meaning mistake in putting herbs into the pot of stew. Reflect on the times when God has set aside our mistakes and still accomplished His purpose. How does that make us feel about our place in the work of God?

9. The last phrase in the chapter is 'according to the Word of the LORD'. What does that tell us about the way God carries out His work?

5

GREAT GOD OF WONDERS (5)

Introduction

Here is one of the Bible's great stories: a crisp and exciting plot with unexpected twists and finely drawn characters. The story begins and ends with a leper and in between lots of expectations and prejudices are overturned. It also returns to the world of power politics after the unknowns of chapter 4 and continues the overall thrust of the Elijah/Elisha narratives in their nationwide, indeed now international, ministry.

There are big theological issues here as well. How does Yahweh relate to other nations not least when they become involved with His people? Again the uneasy relationship between king and prophet is highlighted. The sovereignty of God over both the big events and the small issues is also at the heart of the story. It is a story of the wonderful ways of God.

It is a Gospel story of grace reaching out to the stranger and the longest account of the healing and conversion

of a Gentile. The grace which was to take the Gospel to
'Jerusalem, all Judaea and Samaria and the ends of the
earth,' (Acts 1:8) is already at work here.

Listening to the text

Context and structure

Hostilities with Syria had never been far away in the
Elijah/Elisha stories (e.g. 1 Kings 20 and 22) but here there
appears to be an uneasy peace, allowing traffic between
Israel and Syria (although the king of Israel (v. 7) thinks
Naaman's visit is an excuse to provoke a fight). In the
following chapters there are to be further hostilities which
extend well beyond Elisha's time.

The story develops in five movements:

+ God's unexpected ways (5:1-4)

+ An ineffective king (5:5-7)

+ A miraculous healing (5:8-14)

+ The first tentative steps of faith (5:15-19)

+ Misrepresenting grace (5:20-27)

Working through the text

God's unexpected ways (5:1-4)
A number of preconceived ideas are overturned here.
The first is that God always gives victory to His people.
Why did God give victory to Syria? Because His people
had become idolatrous and unbelieving; 'they rebelled and
grieved the Holy Spirit, therefore he turned to be their
enemy and himself fought against them' (Isa. 63:10). This
eventually is to be the explanation for the Exile as is made

clear in Daniel 1:1-2 where Yahweh delivers Jehoiakim into Nebuchadnezzar's hands. God rules over the whole world and punishes unfaithfulness in His own people.

The next preconceived idea is that ordinary people cannot make a difference. The nameless girl, part of the believing remnant, has been kidnapped, probably never to see her home and family again. She seems to have been well treated but it was not home and she must often have wondered why she was there. Yet she is the vital link in the chain which is to lead to the healing and conversion of the great man in whose house she lives.

The third preconceived idea is that some people have all the luck with everything going for them. Naaman seemed to have it all: position, success, reputation, wealth and courage. Then we read the ominous phrase 'but he was a leper'. This was not necessarily full blown leprosy because the Word can be used of various skin diseases. Yet it was serious and obvious enough to prompt the girl's sympathy and for Naaman to go to great lengths to have it cured.

The fourth preconceived idea is that prophets are all very well for high days and holidays (remember the woman of Shunem's husband in 4:23), but here, as there, he is the one who is able to help and we will soon see the contrast with the king.

An ineffective king (5:5-7)
Unsurprisingly, the king of Syria does not rate an Israelite prophet and sends a letter to the king of Israel (probably still Jehoram – see chapter 3). The usual diplomatic gifts are sent along with a letter which terrifies Jehoram who thinks the king of Syria wants to pick a fight. It is also

likely that he thought a prophet would obviously be a royal
hanger on.

Jehoram (as in chapter 3) is quite happy to use the
language of piety, 'Am I God? Can I kill and bring back
to life?'. However, these are just words to him. The king of
Israel is a politician and can see nothing beyond that realm
(this will be further seen in chapter 6). He, like so many of
his people, knows the right words to say but has no living
faith and no intention of living his life by God's Word.

A miraculous healing (5:8-14)
In any case it is Elisha who takes the initiative and focusses
attention once again on the Word of God – 'that he might
know that there is a prophet in Israel'. Naaman knew
about court prophets and probably imagined that Elisha
was attached to the court and had special magical gifts. But
Elisha is going to show him there is a greater power and in
order to emphasise that it was God and not himself who
was to heal he does not even meet Naaman himself but
sends a messenger telling him to wash in the Jordan. Seven
days is the time prescribed for ritual cleansing from skin
diseases (Lev. 13–14).

Naaman reacts furiously. The 'to me' (v. 11) is emphatic
and shows his pride because Elijah has not reacted the
way the court prophets would have behaved with a magic
gesture and then happily pocketed the money. But it seems
that what the prophet has told him to do is absurd. But
not more absurd than telling people that a man's death on
a cross two thousand years ago brings life to the world.
This is the scandal of the cross in every generation and is a
stumbling block to so many.

The story could have ended there. Naaman could have stormed back to Syria unhealed and unforgiven. But once again the providence of God is at work through unknown people. Naaman's servants, like the girl at the beginning, are more perceptive than Naaman himself. To Naaman's credit, his anger is short-lived and he finds as he obeys that not only is there an outward transformation but that he is a new person.

First tentative steps of faith (5:15-19)
This total change of attitude is seen as he returns humbly and gratefully to Elisha and indeed describes himself as the man of God's servant. He had been healed not by a wave of the hand but by the living God who had shown Himself to be the universal lord. Elisha is also content because it is always the prophetic Word rather than the prophet himself which must be centre stage. There is surely an implied contrast here between the faith of this Syrian and the unbelief in Israel. King Ahaziah (2 Kings 1:3,6 and 16) had believed so little in the God of Israel that he had sent for healing to Baal-Zebub, god of Ekron. Thus this former pagan receives the rich blessings which God's own people had despised.

Some have felt Naaman's conversion is incomplete because of verse 18 where he appears to be saying that far from worshipping Yahweh exclusively he is going to continue to worship Rimmon. 'Rimmon', the thunderer is a name for Baal. Surely we have learned in 1 Kings 18 that we cannot worship Yahweh and Baal. But that is to miss the point. Naaman does not say he will be worshipping Rimmon but that as part of his official duties he has to attend state worship occasions with the king of Syria.

Also he will worship Yahweh on Israelite earth. Again it
is easy to sniff at this and say the Lord can be worshipped
anywhere. However, for this convert returning to paganism
a tangible link with the place of his conversion was vital. It is
unreasonable to expect a new convert to know everything.
In any case the first tentative steps of faith in this man were
so much superior to so much in Israel as to be spectacular.
Indeed, this is what is implied in Jesus' words (Luke 4:27)
which caused His proud listeners to be so angry with Him.
Also Elisha tells Naaman to 'go in peace' which suggests
approval.

Misrepresenting grace (5:20-27)
This final section of the chapter shows Naaman's faith in
an even more striking way by contrast with an unbelieving
Israelite. The story which began with a Gentile healed ends
with an Israelite condemned. What makes this worse is that
Gehazi is not just any Israelite but Elisha's servant who had
seen at first hand the mighty works God did through the
prophet and heard the words he spoke and doubtless many
others privately. Naaman had learned that Yahweh unlike
the pagan gods could not be bribed but Gehazi behaves as
if it was all about money.

Gehazi's offence begins with lightly invoking Yahweh's
name (v. 20) and calling Naaman 'this Syrian' sounds like a
racist jibe. Gehazi tells barefaced lies and is consumed with
covetousness. All that is serious enough but the deadly
thing is his distortion of grace. He misrepresents Yahweh
as a pagan god who can be bought and not only tells lies
but twists the truth about God. This is why the judgment
is so severe. Gehazi is a dreadful warning of the danger of
relying upon anything less than grace.

Gehazi did not understand grace which by its very nature cannot be bought or merited. It shows again how deeply paganism had eaten in to the heart of Israel's faith and how dreadfully the covenant had been misunderstood. This is the difference between religion and the Gospel and is still an issue today.

From text to message

Getting the message clear: the theme
This story is about grace which knows no limits of nationality or background. It is also a story of grace's dark mirror image, the self-centred and deceptive love of possessions and the dire consequences.

Getting the message clear: the aim
This passage challenges so many of our presuppositions, especially our narrow parochialism. The aim is to show the wideness of God's mercy and His amazing grace in unexpected places. It is a story to enlarge our horizons and show us the sovereignty of God over all the nations and to encourage us to see that there is no such thing as a no-go area for the grace of God.

A way in
When I was a child we used to sing a chorus which said:

> Jesus loves the little children,
> All the children of the world.
> Red and yellow, black and white,
> All are precious in his sight.

That is not very good poetry but it is very good theology. The Gospel is international and knows no boundaries. In our preaching we must try to convey the astonishing nature of God's grace reaching right into the enemy camp and transforming an opponent of God's covenant people into a new person.

Ideas for application

+ God's sovereignty over the nations and His hidden work in every part of the world needs to be more prominent in our thinking and preaching. The Gospel hope is not merely the salvation of people (vital and wonderful as that is) but a new heaven and new earth in which is righteousness.

+ The story shows the importance in God's plans of ordinary and unknown people. The young girl here becomes a vital link in the chain which leads to Naaman's conversion. It is worth looking (and perhaps preaching) a series on the unsung heroes of Scripture e.g. the girl here; the unknown Syrian archer used by God to judge wicked Ahab (1 Kings 22:34); the widow at the temple treasury (Luke 21:1-4); Paul's nephew (Acts 23:12-22).

+ Naaman and his wife appear to have been decent pagans and to have treated the young girl well. Two things here: often unconverted people are generous, neighbourly and helpful and we need to thank God for that evidence of common grace. Yet also they need to be converted.

+ We can learn a lot from Elisha's refusal to be overawed by Naaman's celebrity status. Too often we make much of celebrities being converted. Of course we want famous people to come to know the Lord but that is because they are sinners who need salvation not that their status adds to the Gospel.

+ Naaman is a wonderful picture of someone coming to faith. He is angry at first but humble enough to see he is being proud and that he needs to swallow that pride and do what the prophet asks. He is not only healed of his leprosy but comes to know the true God.

+ Elisha's treatment of Naaman is a wonderful example of gentleness and sensitivity with new converts. When someone is converted from paganism we cannot instantly expect a full blown Christian lifestyle. Also we must be aware of the particular difficulties of people in high office who may have to attend in an official capacity events which personally they would rather not.

+ Gehazi is a stark warning of the danger of sinning away our blessings and of failing to respond to the miracle of grace.

Suggestions for preaching

Sermon 1
One way would be to concentrate on the amazing grace of God using some such title as 'Great God of wonders' – this emphasises that the Bible is God's story about God and His concern for the whole world. The main points would be:

· *God continually surprises (5:1-7)*: He does not always give victory to His people; He uses unknown people and the powerful do not always sway events. These kind of considerations help to get under people's radar and make them think.

• *God turns the world upside down (5:8-19)*: The conflict of worldviews where first of all kings are seen as more important than prophets begins this section. Then the importance of being humble and the need to be sensitive with new converts are underlined.

• *God will not tolerate misrepresentation of grace (5:20-27)*: The sad case of Gehazi is about the danger of covetousness and the despising of grace.

This sermon would show the wonders of God's mercy as well as His severity in judging sin.

Sermon 2

This would follow the same broad outlines but focus on the different individuals and their responses:

• The selfless concern of the young girl.

• The political ineptitude and spiritual barrenness of the king of Israel.

• The robust faith and yet gentleness of Elisha.

• The humility and honesty of Naaman.

• The greed and blindness of Gehazi.

This sermon would still place God centre stage but perhaps focus more fully on the human response.

Suggestions for teaching

Questions to help understand the passage

1. How does the author show both the status of Naaman and his vulnerability (5:1)? Why does he do this?

2. What do verses 2-3 suggest about how the young girl is treated? Is this significant for how the story develops?

3. What do verses 4-6 show about the king of Syria's view of who is important In Israel?

4. What does verse 7 tell us about the worldview of the king of Israel?

5. Why does Elisha not meet Naaman in person? (5:8-10)

6. What do we learn about the relationship of Naaman and his servants (5:11-14)? How does that affect our opinion of Naaman?

7. How do we know that more has happened to Naaman than cleansing from leprosy? (5:15)

8. What does Elisha's reply 'Go in peace' (5:19a) show about his assessment of the genuineness of Naaman's faith?

9. What does verse 20 show about Gehazi's attitude to both God and Elisha?

Questions to help apply the passage

1. How does the example of the little girl show us about both the opportunities and cost of evangelism?

2. What do both the kings of Israel and Syria show about their true attitude to God and His prophets? Are there ways in which we are in danger of taking politically expedient actions rather than listening to the Word of God?

3. In what ways can we be over-impressed by celebrities and how can we learn from Elisha's attitude to Naaman? Naaman has shown genuine repentance and faith. How do we show genuine sensitivity as new converts begin to examine the implications of their conversion?

4. What do we learn from Gehazi about the dangers of despising grace?

6

The God of the Personal and the Political (6 & 7)

Introduction

At first sight the contents of these chapters seem random and with little structure but in fact they show careful planning and strong narrative drive. Already Elisha has been established as a figure concerned with both the individual and the nation and this is underlined here. Elisha's God is supreme in both spheres and these chapters unfold different views of reality and of looking at the world. Our view of God is at stake whether in the panic of Elisha's servant (6:15); the unbelief of the officer (7:2) or the confidence of the man of God himself.

The background is the continuing unbelief of the king of Israel (still Jehoram) and seemingly endless hostilities with Syria. Jehoram sees everything in terms of the outward and political and the thrust of the narrative is to show that the 'visionary' prophet is far more effective than the 'pragmatic' king.

Listening to the text

Context and Structure

Events are now moving inexorably to the downfall of
Ahab's house. Back in 1 Kings 21:29, Yahweh had said
to Elijah that judgment would fall on the godless dynasty
in the reign of Ahab's son. Now in the reign of Jehoram
that judgment would be carried out and the blow falls
in Chapters 9 and 10. Like his father, Jehoram is given
numerous opportunities to repent but carries on regardless.

Elisha is now firmly at the centre of the national stage.
Doubtless his dealings with Naaman (chapter 5) had
enhanced his prestige. Yet he is no celebrity, using his
position for his own advantage, but remains concerned for
everyone and for the whole of life.

The story develops in a number of scenes:

+   God's concern for the everyday (6:1-7)

+   Seeing Him who is invisible (6:8-23)

+   The helpless words of humans (6:24-33)

+   The hopeful words of Yahweh (7:1-2)

+   The powerful words of Yahweh (7:3-20)

Working through the text

God's concern for the everyday (6:1-7).
This little episode, apparently trivial, raises a number
of issues. The first thing to notice is 'the company of the
prophets' (v. 1). We read of prophets in 1 Samuel 10:10
and 19:20-21 at the time of Saul who appear to have been
under the authority of Samuel (1 Sam. 19:20). We have
already met the 'community' or 'sons' of the prophets in

1 Kings 20:35; 2 Kings 2:5, 7, 15; 4:1, 38; 5:22. Evidently since 4:38 speaks of them 'sitting at Elisha's feet' he has a teaching role. This is the God-given way of training which Paul is to develop in the Pastoral Letters (see esp. 2 Tim. 2:2). In a later generation we hear of Isaiah's disciples (Isa. 8:16). In 2 Kings 9, it is one of this group who is sent to anoint Jehu.

But here the emphasis is not on their role as learners but on the practicalities of their everyday lives. They need larger accommodation and Elisha is happy to support them in this. The lost axe-head has been subjected to homiletical nonsense of various kinds. For some this has become a moralising tale about not being careless with other people's property. Others have rationalised it and said that Elisha poked around in the water with a stick and pushed the axe-head into shallow water where it could be picked up. Old-fashioned piety allegorises it and sees the axe-head as the human soul sinking in Jordan which represents judgment and the stick is the cross which lifts us out of the waters of death!

What are we to make of it? The first thing to say is that this is a genuine need. After all we can assume that in Jehoram's Israel, such men would not be court favourites and this loss was both a hindrance to the work of building and a debt which would be hard to repay. We are surely grateful for a God who is there for our emergencies small as well as large. (See more in Ideas for application).

The other question is why is this story here? It would have been natural to have followed the story of Naaman with the episode of Elisha at Dothan with its similar emphasis on Israel/Syria relationships. However, God is not only concerned with national generals like Naaman and with the histories of nations. As we saw in chapter 5:2-4, the unnamed little girl played a key part in God's purposes, so here the daily needs of the unnamed prophets matter to Him. He is the God of the personal as well as the political.

Seeing Him who is invisible (6:8-23)

These are words used of Moses and his persevering faith in Hebrews 11:27 and they give us a way into this next episode. The peace following Naaman's healing is short-lived, although these incidents may be grouped thematically rather than chronologically. Here again the focus is on our view of reality. In this story the political and prophetic views of reality clash.

In the first section (vv. 8-13) the emphasis is on the politics of Syria and Israel. As often in narrative, a lot is unsaid. We are not told how Elisha knows the strategy and tactics of the king of Syria. We assume that the king of Israel is Jehoram and that his Syrian counterpart is Ben-hadad but we cannot be certain. Nor do we know how the Syrian officer (v. 12) knows what Elisha knows. This is because the emphasis is less on the individuals than on the attitudes they embody. The narrative is historical but chosen because of what it reveals about the ways of God.

Elisha is happy to give military intelligence to the king of Israel because of his care for the people and obviously the king is happy to take it. Jehoram (if it is he) is always grateful for political and military advice however unwilling to hear the Word of Yahweh through the prophet. The establishment is always happy to use the church if it suits its purpose but reacts angrily when the prophetic Word cuts across its lifestyle.

The king of Syria recognises that Elisha is dangerous and reacts the only way he knows how by sending 'horses and chariots and a strong force' (v. 14). This is a totally over the top reaction; why should all that force be needed to arrest one man? Probably the king was superstitious and feared the powers of the prophet. If this follows chronologically from the Naaman story he would have cause to worry. Indeed, it looks as if Elisha and his servant have no way out.

This is where another view of reality, the prophetic as opposed to the political, comes to the fore. The key lies in comparing verses 15 and 17. Both are about facts: verse 15 about the visible and verse 17 about the invisible. If we confine ourselves to the outward reality then verse 15 is what counts and verse 17 is irrelevant, and indeed this was the young man's fear: 'Oh, my lord, what shall we do?'. So how are we to get to the prophetic reality of verse 17? The answer is in verse 16 'those who are with us are more than those who are with them'.

There are two important issues here. The first is prayer (v. 17a). Notice this is not about prayer changing things, this is about prayer opening eyes to see the reality of God who changes things. Prayer did not create the armies of heaven, it opened the young man's eyes to see them.

And that is the second element: the need for vision. Vision is seeing everything that is there, rather than not there. The visible reality is the armies of Syria, the invisible is the armies of God but it takes the prophetic vision to see past the visible. The prophet does not deny that the armies of Syria are there, rather he points to a far more formidable unseen army. That army is there even when we cannot see it, which is most of the time. We need to rely on the assurance of verse 16 even when the vision of verse 17 is denied us.

But it seems the young man's fears are only too real 'as the enemy came down towards him,' (v. 18) and we are about to see what happens when the visible and invisible realities collide (v. 18). Again Elisha prays but this time it is for blindness for God's enemies. This is not total blindness; the only other time the word is used is in Genesis 19:11 when the Sodomites were trying to break into Lot's house. There, as here, it suggests some kind of visual impairment and confusion which would make the Syrians disorientated. Dothan was some ten miles north of Samaria and the Syrians are easily led there by Elisha who prays again (v. 20) this time for their eyes to be opened. How quickly God can bring human pretensions to nothing.

This is a story of judgment, of the humbling of God's enemies. But it is also a story of grace. The king of Israel has no time for grace but he is rebuked by Elisha and a great feast is prepared for the captured soldiers. We have no way of telling if any of them saw beyond this to the grace of the Gospel but this is a picture of God's enemies welcomed to His table. Ultimately the way of faith which sees the invisible points to true reality.

The helpless words of humans (6:24-33)
The end of the previous incident speaks of the cessation of hostilities from bands of Syrian raiders. This next episode, however, is no guerrilla raid but a full-blown invasion. This invasion causes a desperate famine (v. 25) shown by the horrifically inflated prices: a shekel was the usual wage for a month, so eighty of these for a donkey's head (an unclean animal – see Lev. 11:3) shows that the situation

was humanly hopeless. They are also trading dove dung for a small fortune. Things had gotten so bad. They resort to cannibalism (vv. 28, 29) showing the horrors of war and the total disintegration of life in Samaria. Again, as frequently in narrative, the words show what is at stake.

First there are the hopeless words of humans. There is a cry of help (v. 26) but it is directed to the wrong person. If Jehoram had been the righteous king 'who delivers the needy when they call,' (Ps. 72:12) the cry would have been heeded. Samaria will indeed be saved but not by kings and armies. The king's own words are evasive, again as is his wont, using the language of piety, and here wearing the sackcloth of repentance, but washing his hands of responsibility. Then he resorts to bluster and threats (v. 31). Again, the helplessness of political power is shown by empty and ineffective words.

The hopeful words of Yahweh (7:1-2)

Yahweh now announces through the prophet that relief is on the way. Normal life and business will be resumed the next day. Whether from relief or a sneaking respect for Elisha the king appears to accept that promise. Yet the officer, who wholly lives in the world of visible reality, scorns and rejects the Word from Yahweh. He compounds his unbelief with a cynical reference to 'the floodgates of the heavens' or 'windows of heaven' which are the source of judgment in the Flood (Gen. 7:11) and of blessing for those who respond to God's grace (Mal. 3:10). The Word from heaven comes with judgment or blessing depending on people's response. Here one man's unbelief will not prevent blessing for others but will humble his arrogance.

The powerful words of Yahweh (7:3-20)

An abrupt change of scene now follows as we shift to the city gate and to four lepers. However, this whole section of the narrative in chapters 6 and 7 is about appearance and reality and the ability of God to use the most unlikely instruments to carry out His purpose. The lepers face death whether they stay or go and so choosing the least bad option they decide to go to the Syrian camp and what they find there is astonishing.

The Syrians had fled, leaving food and clothing behind them and this was all Yahweh's doing. 'The Lord had caused,' (v. 6) the Syrians to hear a noise which they thought was foreign armies hired by the king of Israel. The text is emphatic: 'It was the Lord' who caused this panicky flight. Once again the horses and chariots of heaven are in action.

The focus now moves back to the lepers. Unsurprisingly they had partied and squirreled away goodies for themselves, but whether moved by conscience or fear of consequences they decided to share the good news. Typically, the king refuses to believe in spite of Elisha's words to him the previous day. This is unbelief, a persistent refusal to listen to God's Word, not the doubts and wobbles which we all have.

Yet this good news is shared by nameless outcasts. Evangelism has been described as a beggar who has found bread telling others where to find it. This is again gospel grace as we have been given a far greater rescue and have the privilege and responsibility of sharing it with others. Surely the emphasis must be on the message not the messenger, the evangel and not the evangelist. Yahweh's powerful Words of blessing had been proved to be true.

So also, the message of judgment proved to be true 'just as the man of God had foretold' (v. 17). The repetition of the words of verse 2 in verses 19 and 20 underlines the seriousness of rejecting the Word which speaks from heaven (Heb. 12:25) as the officer is condemned out of his own mouth.

From text to message

Getting the message clear: the theme
These stories show a God who is concerned both with individuals and nations. He is active in the visible and invisible worlds and wants us to know that both these worlds are real and that if we confine ourselves to the visible we will not be faithful and effective.

Getting the message clear: the aim
Ultimately these stories are written to encourage faith in God and belief in His providence and are a stark warning to those who are dismissive of His power.

A way in
Since these stories are about appearance and reality and seeing the invisible God, an account I once heard, but cannot precisely reference, about a missionary's experience might prove a good illustration. This happened many years ago in Borneo where a pioneer missionary was working in a remote area much troubled by bandits. His work met with some blessing which angered the bandit chief who had kept the people in subjugation and he threatened to kill the missionary. One night the missionary was far from his base and had to sleep in the open and as he lay down he was conscious of being watched, but he commended himself

to the Lord and slept unharmed. Some time later he met
the bandit chief who said that on the evening in question
they had followed him but had been afraid because he was
guarded by fifteen soldiers. The missionary was puzzled
because he had been alone. He was due to return home
on furlough and he told this story at one of the meetings
he addressed. At the end of the meeting a man came to
him and asked if he could tell precisely when the incident
happened. It emerged said the man that at that time fifteen
people had been praying for the missionary, sensing he
was in danger. Now there is mystery here: what was the
connection between the fifteen people praying in London
and the fifteen soldiers the bandit chief 'saw'? Yet it does
seem as if God sent His angels to protect His servant
(Ps. 91:11). This does not always happen in this way but we
must not become rationalists and limit what God can do.

Ideas for application

+   Some comments on the company of the prophets both
    in terms of training and caring would be appropriate.
    This pattern of mentoring and caring for the needs
    of those in training is a Biblical pattern and a helpful
    reminder of how the Gospel is passed to succeeding
    generations.

+   How do we show we genuinely believe in a God who
    cares both for the everyday and the great moments? We
    rightly warn against becoming trivial and self-obsessed
    in our praying but we need to avoid the opposite
    extreme of apparently despising people's real problems
    and sorrows although they might appear trivial to us.
    The child crying because her dog has died; a teenager in

the first pangs of adolescent love; an old person finding loneliness hard to bear; a busy mother who has lost her keys may not be the stuff of profound theology, but are we not glad that God cares for those things as well as the rise and fall of nations?

+ We need to avoid cynical unbelief like the officer. We rightly deplore those who want endless sensation and miracle but often we lapse into a kind of rationalism which traps God into what we can easily imagine. We need to plan for possibilities and pray for miracles.

+ Both grace and judgment must be at the heart of our message. We can never over-emphasise grace but we can be guilty of cheapening it and divorcing it from the cross and the need for repentance. Similarly, we need to see judgment as grace offering the chance to turn back to God.

+ Above all we need to preach Christ the Word made flesh who cared for the outcast, healed the leper and brought life and immortality to light. Like Elisha He could have called on the armies of heaven: 'Do you think I cannot call on my Father, and he will at once put at my disposal more than twelve legions of angels?' (Matt. 26:53). Yet He chose not to because only by the Cross could He carry out the Father's purpose and ensure heavenly protection for all who believe in Him.

Suggestions for preaching

We would probably want to preach two sermons on these *chapters*. It would be possible to preach three if we devote

one to 6:1-7. See Ralph Davis' marvellous tour de force –
When God Gave the Preacher the Axe.[1]

Alternatively, we could use this as an introduction to
the story of Elisha at Dothan.

Sermon 1

This would use the title already suggested in the exposition
Seeing Him who is invisible and would treat 6:1-23 as one
unit focussing on views of reality and the seen and unseen
worlds. We could treat 6:1-7 as the introduction and
show how its concerns with nameless people and everyday
incidents tell us about the God who cares both for the
personal and the political. Then the main body of the
sermon would develop three views of reality.

The political view of reality (6:8-14)

Both kings view the world through purely political
spectacles, with a dash of superstition. They see diplomacy
or force as the only way to operate. There is the absurdity
of sending an army to capture one man.

The prophet's view of reality (6:15-17)

Key is comparison of verses 15 and 17: both deal with
facts but those of verse 15 are visible and those of verse 17
invisible. The prophet, unlike the kings, is aware of both.

+ Need for prayer – not to create the armies of heaven
  but to see they are there.

+ Need for vision – to be aware of both seen and unseen.

+ Most of the time we do not see the armies of heaven
  and have to trust the words of verse 16.

---

1. Dale Ralph Davis, *2 Kings: The Power and the Fury*; (Christian
   Focus, Fearn, Ross-shire,2005), pp. 101-8.

What happens when those views of reality clash? (6:18-23)
Again the prayers of Elisha both to close and open eyes.

+   God's enemies are humbled – befuddled and helpless.

+   God's enemies receive His grace – a feast instead of a
    massacre.

This sermon shows that the view of the unseen world is the
way to be effective in the seen world (Heb. 11:1).

Sermon 2

This takes the story of invasion and famine (6:24–7:20)
and emphasises the contrast of divine and human words
under the title *The ineffective words of humans and the
powerful words of God*. Not all human words are ineffective
and certainly not when they are the words of the man of
God but many are especially when they express unbelief
and unreality.

The helpless words of humans (6:24-33)
The situation is desperate: war and accompanying famine
and horrors such as cannibalism.

+   Cry for help (v. 26) – but to the wrong person, a godless
    king.

+   Evasive words (v. 27) – king although wearing sackcloth
    knows nothing of genuine repentance.

+   Threatening words (v. 31) – king wants to destroy the
    only one who can help.

The hopeful words of Yahweh (7:1-2)

+   Promise of help (v. 1).

+   Word of judgment (v. 2).

The proof of Yahweh's Word (7:3-20)

+ Nameless outcasts announce the good news.

+ The prophetic Word fulfilled in both judgment and blessing.

Suggestions for teaching

Questions to help understand the passage

1. What does 6:1-7 show about the growth of prophetic activity in Israel both in terms of teaching and care?

2. How does 6:8-12 show that God still protects His faithless people?

3. How does 6:17 authenticate Elisha's ministry? You might like to look again at 2:11.

4. What does 6:21 reveal about the attitude and worldview of the king of Israel?

5. How do we reconcile 6:23b and 6:24?

6. What does the famine in 6:25 show about God's judgment? It would be useful to look at Leviticus 26:27-29 and Deuteronomy 28:52-57.

7. What does 7:2 show about the importance of believing Yahweh's Word?

8. Why does the king of Israel suspect a trap? (7:12)

9. How do we know from 7:19-20 that Elisha is a true prophet?

Questions to help apply the passage

1. What does the incident in 6:1-7 show about the things that matter to God?

2. Does God still protect His people even when they are being unfaithful? You may want to look at both communal and personal matters.

3. How do we hold on to the faith of 6:16 when the sight of God's armies in 6:17 is denied to us?

4. What does 6:23 show us about the grace of God?

5. Why is the king of Israel powerless to help (6:27)? It might be useful to consider how often we resort to worldly methods when the way of faith seems not to be working.

6. How do we recognise the difference between cynical unbelief (7:2) and genuine lament and protest? You may want to look at Psalm 95 with its condemnation of whingeing unbelief and Psalms such as 77 and 88 with their puzzled but still believing protest.

7. What do the lepers show about spreading the good news? Particularly look at how they enjoy it themselves and then are motivated to share it with others.

8. 7:17-20 demonstrate both grace and judgment. Are there ways in which we sometimes present a truncated gospel which fails either to rejoice in God's amazing grace or tremble at His just judgment?

7

The Kindness and Sterness of God (8)

Introduction

These words from Romans 11:22 sum up neatly the issues raised in this, and indeed the following chapter. Here we are to have one of the last glimpses of Elisha especially in national affairs. Also the long prophesied judgment on Ahab's house draws nearer, and this is one of the reasons why the story returns to Judah and the consequences of the entanglement of Jehoshaphat's family with Ahab's family.

In a way which has become familiar, Elisha moves easily in different layers of society and indeed goes on a visit to the King of Syria. The interplay between prophetic words and political situations is again powerfully underlined.

Listening to the text

Context and Structure

The narrative returns to the woman of 4:8-37 and to another glimpse of God's grace in action. At that time she had not needed any help, 'I have a home among my own people' (4:13), but now she gratefully accepts the warning to move because of coming famine. As often, in the Elisha stories, the chronology is uncertain, not least in the mention of Gehazi. However, the chapter is again emphasising Elisha's continuing involvement in individual, national and international affairs. God behind the scenes is working out His purpose.

The narrative unfolds in three sections:

+ God is the Lord of life (8:1-6)

+ God and the nations (8:7-15)

+ God and the covenant people (8:16-29)

Working through the text

God is the Lord of Life (8:1-6)
This little episode (like the lost axe-head in 6:1-7) is no space-filler but another evidence of the grace evident in Elisha's ministry which reflects the grace of the Lord Himself. The key phrase is 'restored to life' (once in v. 1 and three times in v. 5). In a link with the next section, a form of the same verb is used in verses 8, 9, 10, 14 where Ben-Hadad asks if he will 'recover', be restored, from his illness. The emphasis here is on Yahweh as Lord of life.

His care for the physical welfare of His people is evident here; recalling his provision for Elijah in 1 Kings 17. Similarly, unexpected means are used here as the woman and her family take refuge in the land of the old enemy, the Philistines. Again the importance of obedience to the Word of God is underlined: 'The woman proceeded to do as the man of God said' (v. 2).

The famine ends and the woman returns and asks the king for her land. The king (probably still Jehoram) is curiously asking Gehazi about 'the great things Elisha had done' (v. 4). His interest, like that of Herod in John the Baptist, was a desire for a good story and did not lead to saving faith. In any case he does restore the woman's land, perhaps because of his fear of Elisha.

The mention of Gehazi here is puzzling after his dismissal and leprosy in 5:27. As already noticed the Elisha stories are topical rather than chronological and this could be earlier than the events of chapter 5. In any case this episode shows that Jehoram is persuaded by evidence of the grace and power of Yahweh but continues his own way.

God and the nations (8:7-15)

Before examining this section it would be helpful to reread 1 Kings 19:15-18 where Yahweh tells Elijah to anoint Hazael king over Aram, Jehu as king of Israel and Elisha to succeed him as prophet. As was pointed out in the exposition of that passage in the previous volume, it is unfair to criticise Elijah for carrying out only the anointing of Elisha because it is the Word of God and not the messenger which has the power. Indeed, in chapter 9 it is one of 'the company of prophets', not Elisha personally who anoints Jehu. As Daniel puts it: 'He changes times and seasons, he removes kings and sets up kings' (Dan. 2:21). Here the emphasis is on God the Judge, the Lord of the nations.

We are not told the reason for Elisha's visit to Damascus but the point is that the words first given to Elijah back in 1 Kings 19 are now beginning to be fulfilled. Verse 10 is puzzling because Elisha appears to be dishonest with Ben-Hadad by saying he will recover. But this could mean that left to the normal processes of healing he would indeed get better but something else is going to intervene. Hazael, like Macbeth hearing he was to be king, decides to give providence a helping hand.

More importantly, these verses show us a theology of history. The judgment will come and bring war with all its attendant horrors (v. 12). God will punish His people by giving them over to their enemies who will devour them. However, these enemies will themselves be punished for their arrogance and cruelty. Isaiah makes a similar point about Assyria 'the rod of my anger' (Isa. 10:5). God does not underwrite brutality and evil but in the fallen world uses human means to carry out His purposes. Thus the prophet weeps at the thought of the horrors to come as Jesus wept over Jerusalem (Luke 19:41). The Lord does not desire the death of the wicked.

Hazael gives Ben-Hadad the first of Elisha's messages but not the second and probably (the details of v. 15 are obscure) smothers the king. He then takes power. Grace in verses 1-6 and judgment in verses 7-15 are part of the same message.

God and the covenant people (8:16-29)
Now for the first time since 1 Kings 22:41-50, which describe the reign of Jehoshaphat, we return to Judah and to the unfortunate consequences of that king's fascination with Ahab and his family. Joram or Jehoram, same name as the Israelite king, initiates an evil and idolatrous reign, no doubt aided and abetted by his wife, a daughter of Ahab and Jezebel. It is more than his name that this king of Judah shares with his Israelite counterpart. It is a striking example of how compromise in one generation can lead

to apostasy in the next. Jehoshaphat, for all his weakness, remained faithful to Yahweh; his descendants however descend into idolatry.

Verse 19, though, brings back to light the promise of the inextinguishable lamp (1 Kings 11:36; 15:4). This plan has not been derailed by a king who is entwined with Ahab's dynasty. This covenant is not simply about the future of Judah but about the redemption of the world and the coming of God's kingdom.

Yet Jehoram of Judah has warnings in the rebellion of Edom and Libnah. King Jehoram escapes with his life but the loss of Edom would mean not just hurt pride but the interruption of caravan trade with Arabia. In many ways the revolt of Libnah was more ominous as it was a Judaean city south-west of Jerusalem. To have a dissenting province so close to home would be an affront. Again we see the Lord of the nations at work.

Ahaziah, Jehoram's son, was no improvement on his father and again his apostasy is traced to his link with Ahab's family (v. 27). His mother, Jehoram's wife, was Athaliah, a name to loom ominously until after chapter 11. The repetition of 'the house of Ahab' is a deliberate contrast to 'the house of David'. Ahaziah ultimately reigned for a mere twelve months. Echoes of Jehoshaphat (v. 28) appear again in Ramoth Gilead (remember 1 Kings 22). In any case, Israelite King Jehoram is wounded and Ahaziah pays him a visit, no doubt to commiserate. Probably this implies that Ahaziah had sent troops to Ramoth Gilead rather than gone personally. In any case neither the royal convalescent nor his royal visitor had the least inkling of the major events that were about to unfold. The shadows are gathering around the house of Ahab and soon it will disappear unloved and unlamented.

From text to message

Getting the message clear: the theme
This collection of stories is about a God who is both rich in mercy and just in judgment. This theme is worked out both in private conversations and public ways.

Getting the message clear: the aim
This chapter shows that God works out His purposes whether in judgment or mercy; it shows that faithfulness is ultimately rewarded and disobedience ultimately punished.

A way in
This chapter, like many in Kings, shows a recognition that the Gospel is public truth. It is not simply about individual response but about the whole of life, about nations and communities. Wisdom utters her voice in the public squares and streets and in the gateways of the city (Prov. 1:20-21). This does not mean that we make political and social judgments in our sermons on matters on which the Bible is silent, matters on which we have no more authority than anyone else. It does mean, however, that we teach the doctrine of providence which governs the rise and fall of nations and not just our personal and church lives. We need a robust theology of history and a trust that all events, however dire, are caught up in God's purpose to bring in the kingdom which will never end.

Ideas for application

+ God protects His people in unexpected ways such as providing shelter for this woman and her family in the land of the Philistines, the ancient enemy. This is applied to all God's people in Revelation 12:14 where the woman (Zion) hides in the desert from the dragon. This in effect is part of the doctrine of creation in that nowhere is out of God's control (see also Ps. 139:7-10).

+ It is possible to be fascinated by stories of God's work as Jehoram is (v. 3) but for that to be mere curiosity and not a sign of saving faith. Miracles do not in themselves convince unbelievers.

+ The Word of God does not lose its power over the years when we compare verses 7-15 with 1 Kings 19:15-18. This encourages us to keep going when there is little sign of success.

+ The brief notices of the kings of Judah (vv. 16-29) illustrate the danger of compromising alliances. Error seldom comes immediately but compromise sows deadly seeds for the future. Francis Schaeffer used to ask of suspect teaching; '*What effect will this have on our grandchildren?*'

+ God is faithful to His covenant and Judah has not yet passed the point of no return, but the time will come (see 2 Kings 21:10-15).

Suggestions for preaching

The chapter could be preached as a whole, following the lines suggested in the exposition.

The kindness and sternness of God

The introduction would focus on the hand of God behind the scenes in both private and public matters:

God is Lord of life (vv. 1-6)

+ He cares for physical needs.

+ He does great things.

+ He cares for His servants.

God is Lord of the nations (vv. 7-15)

+ His Word challenges nations as well as individuals.

+ The prophetic Word sets the events in motion.

God and the covenant people (vv. 16-29)

+ Events flow from unwise decisions by Jehoshaphat (1 Kings 22).

+ God is faithful to His covenant.

+ God brings about events to teach His people lessons.

Suggestions for Teaching

Questions to help understand the passage

1. Reread chapter 4 and consider why Elisha still takes an interest in this woman and what it reveals about his ministry.

2. What does the mention of Gehazi tell us about the probable arrangement of the Elisha stories?

3. Is the king sincere in his desire to hear about 'the great things Elisha has done'?

4. What do we learn about Elisha's attitude to the sinful people of Israel in verse 12?

5. Why does the narrative return to Judah in verses 16-29? You might like to reread 1 Kings 22.

6. Why is the 'house of Ahab' mentioned several times (vv. 18, 27)?

Questions to help apply the passage

1. What does the first story (8:1-6) show about both the power and tenderness of God?

2. How does the incident of Elisha and Hazael show us how to preach judgment without being judgmental?

3. What does that incident also reveal about the prophetic Word? You would probably want to read 1 Kings 19 again.

4. How do we reconcile God's faithfulness to His people in spite of their continued sin? It would be useful to read 2 Samuel 7:12-16.

5. Do these brief notes about the kings of Judah help us to see the dangers and consequences of compromise?

8

Judgment at Last (9)

Introduction

The long announced judgment on Ahab's house now unfolds with astonishing speed in this and the next chapter. The anointing of Jehu as king of Israel had been told to Elijah but he had been unable to carry this out and, in the event, it is not done by Elisha but one of the company of the prophets. This was no failure on the part of Elisha but a demonstration that the Word, not the speaker, is what matters and the action is carried out by a disciple of Elisha. (See commentary on 1 Kings 19.)

For much of the preceding narrative God has been active behind the scenes as this godless dynasty continues to dig its own grave but now His judgment is to take centre stage, and just as Elisha had carried out the command to announce that Hazael is to be King of Syria, so now Jehu and a new dynasty is to come to the throne of the northern kingdom, Israel.

It is worth looking at the chronology at this point. Ahab's dynasty had reigned for thirty and more years. In 1 Kings 16:29 we are told that Ahab reigned for twenty-two years; Ahaziah for two years (1 Kings 22:51); Jehoram for twelve years (2 Kings 8:25). Indeed, if we add the twelve years of Omri, Ahab's father (1 Kings 16:23) the dynasty lasted nearly half a century. During that time there were abundant opportunities to repent, showing that Yahweh is indeed slow to anger (Exod. 34:6). We are reminded of the Herods in the New Testament, a family at whose doors grace knocked regularly but who chose the path of worldly power.

That is always an important lesson to be learned in every age. The United Kingdom has had centuries of the Gospel and not only the spiritual root but the fruit, the social blessings which have flowed from it. Hospitals, schools, social reforms and care for people are all gifts which much of our society forget came from the planting of the Gospel in our society. We are in grave danger of sinning away these blessings. Here the time for repentance is over and the axe falls on the godless family.

Listening to the text

Context and structure

At the beginning of the chapter Jehoram is still king but meets his end in verse 24 and Jehu, first mentioned in 1 Kings 19:15-18, is to accede to the throne of Israel. At last Israel will be free from Ahab's house and in the next chapter freed, at least temporarily, from Baal worship. This is a roller coaster of a chapter full of violent action and the leisurely Jehoram narrative is replaced by the equivalent of a tidal wave.

The story develops in three scenes

+ A dramatic anointing (9:1-13)

+ Blood and vengeance (9:14-29)

+ Exit Jezebel (9:30-37)

Working through the text

A dramatic anointing (9:1-13)

The initiative is with Elisha, or rather God working through Elisha as he sends an unnamed prophet to anoint Jehu. Jehoshaphat is not, of course the former king of Judah, and since Jehu is simply called 'son of Nimshi' (v. 14) it is probable his grandfather was a well-known figure. In any case he is a prominent army officer. Jehu is in fact the only northern king recorded to have been anointed.

The message given by Elisha is brief and refers only to the anointing and not the reasons for it. Some have argued that the prophet himself embellished this in verses 6-10 but that is to show literary insensitivity. Verse 3 gives us the summary of the message and then the full message is developed at the climax of the story. Also implied is the authority of the Word which Jehu fails to question. It seems likely that Jehu was motivated by personal ambition and probably a genuine desire to put right the problems Jehoram had failed to deal with. After all, the king had scarcely been successful in the wars with Syria and then add the frequent times of famine, it is likely that there had been grumbling and even plotting among the army top brass. The kingdom was ripe for change and the longing for a strong leader was doubtless a factor in this.

However, we are left in no doubt that while these human factors were important, it is the Word of God which sets these events in motion. Notice the repetition of 'I' in verses 6-9 outlining the judgments on both Ahab and Jezebel. We are also reminded that this judgment is just and has already been exemplified in the judgment on the house of Jeroboam and then Baasha (1 Kings 14:14; 15:25-31). God will avenge His suffering people.

The rest of the army officers accept Jehu's anointing without question even if they think the prophet is a madman and this speaks volumes for his prestige and tends to confirm the suspicion that they were disillusioned with the present regime. Thus suddenly the whole situation changes which does happen every so often in politics. At the time of writing the vote of the United Kingdom in June 2016 to leave the European Union is already affecting the political life of the nation in totally unexpected ways and doubtless will continue to do so.

Blood and vengeance (9:14-29)

Jehu wastes no time in carrying out the prophetic Word. Indeed the words 'he drives like a madman' (v. 20) is probably an index to his personality and way of working. We are reminded of the national situation and the ominous mention of Ramoth Gilead (v. 14) echoes the death of Ahab and anticipates the death of Jehoram. We are further reminded that Ahaziah of Judah is visiting Jehoram in Jezreel (v. 16). At that moment Jehoram does not know about the crowning of Jehu, but hearing that Jehu's troops were on the way he sends out two messengers to find out what is happening, and when they fail to return goes out himself to meet Jehu. This meeting proves fatal to him and to Ahaziah of Judah. Judgment falls on Judah as well because of Ahaziah's foolish linking with Jehoram. It is an exciting episode but is there more to it than that?

There are numerous echoes of earlier passages which confirm the justice of what happens here and a reminder of the death of Ahab, shot by an arrow (1 Kings 22:34) and the death of Ahaziah of Judah , not as fortunate as Jehoshaphat (1 Kings 22:32-33). See further comments in chapter 11 on the whole sad story of Jehoshaphat's family and their association with the house of Ahab.

Also the mention of the idolatry and witchcraft of Jezebel (v. 22) is significant. The reign of Ahab and Jezebel had been especially marked by the worship of Baal, imported from Jezebel's homeland, and this had caused famine, death and now judgment. Thus there could be no peace. Jehoram, throughout his story, had shown himself to be a politician for whom peace and justice meant a situation where he could carry on his sweet way and ignore Yahweh's prophets. But peace which ignored the covenant and dethroned Yahweh could only ever be illusory.

A further and specific judgment occurs when Jehoram's body is thrown into Naboth's vineyard and a further detail is added to the story of 1 Kings 21. We learn now that not only did Jezebel have Naboth murdered, she had his sons killed as well. The fate of His people is known in detail and not just in general terms to the Lord.

Ahaziah, King of Judah, first escapes but is eventually killed as well. In so many ways this association with Ahab had led the family of Jehoshaphat to be feckless followers rather than taking a strong lead. We again fear for the line of David and this is to emerge powerfully again in chapter 11, but God is on the throne and working through these political and military episodes.

Exit Jezebel (9:30-37)
The foxes have gone but the vixen remains and the spotlight falls on Jezebel who, haughty to the end, confronts Jehu. She knows her history, and Jezebel puts on her glad rags, perhaps hoping to come to some kind of arrangement with Jehu, but in any case is determined to go out in style.

Again Jehu acts briskly and Jezebel's end is swift and horrible and the body which she had taken such pains to make beautiful becomes a few fragments trampled by horses and eaten by dogs. This is not pretty and it is not meant to be. The fate of Jezebel, like that of Daniel's accusers (Dan. 6:24), shows how dreadful judgment can be and warns us not to be sentimental. Rivers of blood had flowed because of this wicked woman's fanatical Baalism and there must have been rejoicing at the end of a tyrannical regime. The prophet Nahum, speaking of the fall of Nineveh and the end of the monstrously cruel Assyrian empire, expresses it thus, 'Everyone who hears the news about you claps his hands at your fall, for who has not felt your endless cruelty?' (Nahum 3:19)

From text to message

Getting the message clear: the theme
The Lord will carry out deserved judgment in His own good time. Years, even centuries may pass, but the Word of judgment will be fulfilled. The lapse of time is not because He is slow to carry out His Word but because He does not want the death of anyone but is patient and calls people to repentance.

Getting the message clear: the aim

The judgment of God and His rule over history needs to be continually emphasised. It will be challenging, warning us that our God is a consuming fire and it will be encouraging reassuring us that God's kingdom will come.

A way in

Sometimes on news programmes which are describing some violent scenes the newsreader will say something like, 'this contains scenes which some viewers may find distressing'. A similar health warning might be given as we introduce this chapter. It is grim reading and seems to show far more about human savagery than God's grace. Two important considerations follow from this.

The first is that sin and judgment are real and must never be watered down. This is the consistent Biblical picture. After the Fall, the first baby to be born into the world was a murderer and the next baby to be born was his victim. In Genesis 6:12 God says He will put an end to people 'for the earth is filled with violence'. A violent and brutal society is one where all fear of God and compassion for humanity has disappeared. The Bible refuses to be sentimental about humanity and emphasises our accountability to God.

The second is that grace still reaches out to the penitent. The brutal and violent end of Jezebel is a direct result of her own ceaseless cruelty, but all through the years, Ahab's house had heard the voice of God warning them of judgment and calling them to repentance. A sermon on this passage, if it is to be faithful to the text, needs to sound both notes.

Ideas for application

+   The complete reliability of God's Word needs to be prominent in our thinking. This is not easy especially in the many times when nationally, communally and individually there is little to encourage. We need to take a long view and a wide view and not simply look at our own backyard.

+   Related to this is the idea that God's servants will ultimately be vindicated. What happens here is specific to the situation but Jesus applies it more widely in the parable of the unjust judge and the persistent widow (Luke 18:1-8). Justice will come and this judgment anticipates the Last Day.

+   The apparently messy events of history and the mixed motives of its leading participants are all worked into God's overall purpose where one day His will is carried out on earth as well as in heaven. We will all ultimately serve God's purpose, but as C. S. Lewis said, 'It will make all the difference to us whether we serve him the way John did or the way Judas did'.

+   Jezebel dies bravely but this does not mean that her character is thereby redeemed and that in some way she becomes admirable. Suicide bombers die bravely but their actions are despicable. There is no deathbed repentance here.

Suggestions for preaching

Probably it would be best to take the chapter as a whole for it is a continuous story.

Sermon 1

We could follow the flow of the narrative with the three suggested divisions:

The prophetic Word fulfilled (9:1-14)

+ The Word fulfilled decades after it was spoken (see 1 Kings 19).

+ The justice of God's judgment.

The violence which results (9:15-29)

+ Violence not good but God overrules it.

+ Echoes of death of Ahab and involvement of Jehoshaphat's family – danger of compromise with evil.

The arch-persecutor removed (9:30-37)

+ God vindicates His suffering people.

+ A brave death does not compensate for an unrepentant life.

Sermon 2

A more thematic approach would focus on the underlying theology:

God is slow to anger

+ Point out that for nearly fifty years the Omri/Ahab dynasty had ruled.

+ God had given many chances to repent.

+ Grace had been rejected.

God is swift to judge

+   Not a contradiction of the above rather that when judgment comes it unfolds.

+   The prophetic Word is fulfilled.

+   Human drama unfolds.

God's servants will be vindicated

+   God honours His Word.

+   God removes the arch-persecutor.

+   At the end of chapter 10 a suggested outline will be given for preaching chapters 9 and 10 together.

Suggestions for teaching

Questions to help understand the passage

1. Why does Elisha urge the young prophet to be swift in his action?

2. What do verses 6-10 tell us about the fulfilment of God's Word? (It would be useful to read again 1 Kings 19:15-18.)

3. Why is Ramoth Gilead important? (Read 1 Kings 22 again.)

4. How is the authority and vigour of Jehu emphasised? (e.g. vv. 13 and 20)

5. Why is it appropriate that Jehoram should end up in Naboth's vineyard (v. 26)? Read again 1 Kings 21.

6. How has Ahaziah of Judah become involved?

7. How does Jezebel face her death?

8. How does her death fulfil prophecy?

Questions to help apply the passage

1. How do verses 1-9 show that the Word of God will be fulfilled and that it is the message and not the messenger which is important? In what ways will that affect our attitude towards preaching today?

2. How do the echoes of Ahab's death and Jehoshaphat's unfortunate involvement with him (1 Kings 22) help us to see the danger of compromising with God's enemies?

3. What does verse 22 teach about the importance of righteousness in a truly peaceful nation?

4. How does the chapter show us that God's servants will be vindicated and His enemies destroyed?

5. How does a chapter like this prevent us from being sentimental about the Gospel?

9

THE END OF A GODLESS FAMILY (10)

Introduction

The judgment which had fallen on individuals now falls on the whole of Ahab's family and it is a violent purge. This is the kind of passage often seen as typical of the Old Testament with a violent and bloodthirsty God who is contrasted with the gentle Jesus of the New Testament. Two things need to be remembered. The first is that most of the teaching on judgment in the New Testament comes from the Lord Jesus Christ Himself (see e.g. Matt. 13:40-42; Luke 11:29-32; 16:19-31). The second is that Ahab's house had been repeatedly warned by Elijah and Elisha and others, yet had failed to heed the call to repent. As long as that godless family remained there could be no peace and justice.

Jehu is the chosen instrument and he sets about the task with relish. Seventy sons, the extended family of Ahab, are targeted. This may be a round figure like Jacob's descendants in Egypt (Gen. 46:27); in any case the purge is to be thorough.[1]

Decisive action is also to be taken against Baal-worship and both its priests and temple are to be destroyed. However, Jeroboam's bull gods remain and the purge, while thorough, does not restore the worship of Yahweh in Israel. This is the end of nearly fifty years of Omri's dynasty (see comments on chapter 9) and the possibility of a new start. Back in 1 Kings, the prophet Ahijah had told Jeroboam that if he followed Yahweh his dynasty would be as lasting as David's (1 Kings 11:38). That opportunity had not been taken and here Jehu is also to fail to seize the moment (vv. 30-31).

Listening to the text

Context and structure

Although Jehu was to reign for twenty-eight years (v. 36), little is said about that time other than recounting the destruction of Ahab's house, and the dismantling of Baalism in Israel, which is his real place in the story. Even in this he delivers only half of what he should have (vv. 30-31) and in spite of his reputation as a war lord, he fails to deal with the resurgent threat of Syria.

The story develops in five movements.

+ The end of Ahab's house (10:1-11)

+ Continuing danger to Judah (10:12-14)

+ A conservative response (10:15-17)

+ Destruction of Baal-worship (10:18-27)

+ Jehu found wanting (10:28-36)

---

1.   See Wiseman pp 224-25.

Working through the text

The end of Ahab's house (10:1-11)
Ahab's supporters were still around; they may well have hurried to Samaria after seeing Jehu's activities in Jezreel.[2] Jehu sends letters to test their mettle and indeed their loyalty to the old regime. After all, they are spoiled for choice for a king to replace Jehoram (v. 3). However, they are totally intimidated and send a message of grovelling submission to Jehu (v. 3). Jehu is not to be fobbed off and insists on the heads of Ahab's sons as a test of the loyalty they profess. The grisly act is carried out and the heads duly arrive in baskets. Here is another classic example of Hebrew narrative; succinct, crisp and realistic.

Jehu is a politician as well as a warlord and he distances himself from the slaughter of the seventy (v. 9). He uses the language of piety (v. 10). This neatly sums up the theology of the passage. What Jehu says is true; Elijah had prophesied the end of Ahab's line and the bloodthirsty activities of chapters 9 and 10 had carried this out. God is using Jehu, a flawed instrument, to do this but that does not mean that Jehu is a godly man (v. 31) and it is difficult not to see his bloodthirsty nature revealed here. Judgment is not pleasant but it is necessary to remove evil.

Continuing danger to Judah (10:12-14)
Ahaziah of Judah, unwisely associating with Jehoram of Israel, had already been fatally wounded by Jehu's archers (9:27-28) and it may be that this contingent from Judah were as yet unaware of Jehu's activities. In any case their naivety in claiming friendship with Ahab's house is their

---

2.   See Davis p. 158 n.2.

undoing and they suffer the same fate as the sons of Ahab. There is much left unsaid here; the location of Beth Eked is unknown as is the true reason for this Judaean delegation. Jehu would undoubtedly be aware of a pro-Ahab faction in Judah and would welcome the chance to get rid of at least some of them. Perhaps he wanted to take over Judah as well.

Some have seen this as an irrelevant insertion contributing nothing of significance to the story but that is not the case. The fate of Judah, especially its royal house, heirs to the promises to David is central to the overall narrative of Kings. Chapter 11 is to see a most determined and all but successful attempt to eliminate the house of David and we are reminded of the fragility of that house at this moment not least with a ruthless man like Jehu on the throne in the north.

A conservative response (10:15-17)

Jehu wants to win support and the opportunity presents itself as he meets Jehonadab. His descendants, the Rechabites, appear in Jeremiah 35 where they say that their ancestor (there called Jonadab) taught them to be teetotal and embrace a nomadic lifestyle (Jer. 35:6-7). Since they represented what we might call conservative Yahwism, Jehu professes his zeal for Yahweh and sees them as useful allies in the attack on Baalism he is about to mount. Thus Jehu enlists Jehonadab as a key ally (v. 23).

Verse 17 is a summary statement reminding us that the political purge had happened. Yet it is not ultimately Jehu's doing. As so often in the story the driving force is the Word of Yahweh through the prophet.

Destruction of Baal-worship (10:18-27)

The political establishment associated with Ahab had been wiped out but the religious establishment looked as strong as ever particularly when Jehu said that his zeal for Baal would exceed that of Ahab. The repetition of 'Baal', seventeen times in verses 18-28 seems to underline the entrenched domination of the god and the impossibility of ousting him. Initially the parade of the priests of Baal in their robes would be designed to look impressive and intimidating to those who had not bowed the knee to Baal.

At first the liturgy proceeds as normal with sacrifices and burnt offerings with Jehu himself presiding. But this is soon overwhelmed by the eighty soldiers who kill the priests and then enter the inner shrine of the temple and destroy the sacred stone. The temple is not only destroyed but suffers the ultimate humiliation of being used as a public toilet. Essentially idolatry is ridiculous, a point later emphasised by Isaiah as he mocks both the making and worship of idols (Isa. 44:12-20).

What Jehu did was certainly in line with the words of Moses about idolatry in Deuteronomy 13. However, the next verses tend to suggest that it was detestation of Ahab rather than love for Yahweh which was his main motivation. Baal-worship had been a key part of Ahab's dynastic policy and its elimination would further remove any lingering loyalty to that family.

Jehu found wanting (10:28-36).

The time has come for the overall assessment of Jehu. The destruction of Baal-worship was indeed to his credit as the summary verse 28 makes clear. Since 1 Kings 16:31-32 the narrative has concentrated on Baalism and its deadly threat to the life of Israel. However, the figure of Jeroboam, the first king of the northern kingdom, has haunted the story with his epithet that he 'caused Israel to sin'. The syncretism he introduced (see comments in *Teaching 1 Kings* pp. 181-2) was alive and well. Removing the worst kind of idolatry does not mean that other types of idolatry can be tolerated. This lends some support to the view that Jehu was anti Ahab rather than pro Yahweh. Indeed none of the northern kings was to introduce a wholesale purge of idolatry.

Verses 30 and 31 give a balanced picture. He did what was right in eradicating Ahab's house and for that was rewarded by the promise of a dynasty that would last four generations. This was over one hundred years and the kings concerned were Jehoahaz, Joash, Jeroboam II and Zechariah. (2 Kings 15:12). This shows how dreadful Ahab's house had been and how praiseworthy it was to get rid of it.[3]

Verse 31 shows the true state of Jehu's heart and his mixed motives. Jehu had indeed overthrown Baalism but left untouched the idolatry which had allowed it to take root. The heart has already been seen to be important, notably with Solomon whose 'heart was not fully devoted to the LORD his God' (1 Kings 11:4). Because of this, the revolution of Jehu remained an external one which in no way impeded the slide to eventual exile in Assyria.

---

3.   Why then does Yahweh say, 'I will punish the house of Jehu for the massacre at Jezreel'? (Hosea 1:4) Presumably because Jehu had exceeded his commission in his bloodthirstiness, his failure to restore the worship of Yahweh and the lack of any scruple. Thus like Ahab's dynasty, Jehu's dynasty would come to a bloody end.

This failure of true faith also echoes what happened in the closing years of Solomon's reign. Failure in true allegiance to Yahweh is reflected in Yahweh bringing foreign enemies to reduce the size of the kingdom. Hazael of Syria (as predicted in 8:12-13) was now unleashed.[4] Some of that territory was to be regained by Jeroboam II (14:25) but it was an ominous sign of things to come. Hazael, as much as Jehu, was an instrument of God's judgment.

Jehu had fulfilled his purpose in the elimination of Ahab's house and there is not much more to be said. He is credited with 'achievements' (v. 34) but no hint is given of what these were. We do know that he paid tribute to the Assyrians.[5] However, the rest of the twenty-eight years is passed over in silence.

From text to message

Getting the message clear: the theme
The main emphasis is that God will use often unworthy people for His good purposes. We live in a fallen world and in the affairs of nations often motives and actions which are not good in themselves are used to bring about God's will. The words of Joseph to his brothers, 'you meant it for evil but God meant it for good' (Gen. 50:20) not only apply to that situation but to God's overall dealings with a sinful world.

---

4. This coincided with a time when the rising power of Assyria was dealing with problems nearer home.

5. The 'Black Obelisk ' of the Assyrian king Shalmaneser 111 portrays Jehu bowing before the king as he pays tribute. Ironically Jehu is described as from 'the land of Omri'. How differently the Bible and the powers of the time see history!

Getting the message clear: the aim

To show that because at some time and in some way we have done God's will does not mean that we will necessarily continue to do so. We need to guard our heart and examine our motives.

A way in

Often we wonder why there is so much judgment in the Bible. At least part of the reason for this is that we too often confuse God's just judgment with our own judgmentalism. God's anger is slow (Ahab's dynasty had been given half a century); our anger is often injured vanity. Also we tend to think that if we obey God in some things that gives us an excuse to ignore Him in others.

This is not a comfortable message to preach but neither is it a comfortable message to hear as preachers. Indeed, the only way we can avoid preaching judgment without judgmentalism is to realise we are under judgment as well.

Ideas for application

- The need for judgment to bring about the kingdom of God must be realised. This means that at times of apostasy we must look beyond that and believe God is working out His purpose even in the darkest times.

- We need to recognise that in a fallen world the instruments God uses will often be less than ideal. God may use one tyrant to overthrow another, without compromising His own holiness.

- The instruments God uses are nevertheless responsible for their actions and cannot themselves evade judgment. See Isaiah 10:5-34 about how the Lord uses Assyria, the rod of His anger, to punish His rebellious people but they themselves are then destroyed because of their overbearing arrogance. The book of Habakkuk would also make a similar claim.

+   God's Word needs to be obeyed in its entirety. Jeroboam got rid of Baal-worship but kept Jeroboam's sacred bulls. All idolatry is wrong.

+   As so often in Kings it is the heart which matters. Jehu was not devoted to Yahweh and His Word (v. 31). A ruthless iconoclastic zeal is no substitute for humble obedience.

Suggestions for preaching

Sermon 1
This follows the unfolding events of the chapter:

The godless family eliminated (10:1-17)

+   Judgment may be delayed but it cannot be avoided.

+   Judah still in danger because of being too close to Ahab's family.

Godless religion destroyed (10:18-27)

+   The apparent triumph of Baalism.

+   The humiliating end of Baalism.

Danger of half–hearted obedience (10:28-36)

+   Idolatry remains and God's Word not obeyed.

+   Political weakness.

Sermon 2

This would take a more thematic approach:

Yahweh uses flawed instruments for His good purposes

Zeal against evil needs to be accompanied by passion for good

Actions have both spiritual and political consequences

Suggestions for teaching

Questions to help understand the passage

1. How does Jehu show political cunning as well as military power? (vv. 1-8)

2. Why is Jehu keen to associate his actions with the words of Elijah? (v. 10)

3. What is the significance of introducing Judah here? (vv. 12-14)

4. Why does Jehonadab want to be an ally of Jehu? (vv. 15-17)

5. Why do you think the prophets of Baal were so naïve? (vv. 18-27)

6. Why is Jeroboam mentioned at this point? (vv. 29-31)

7. How does the mention of Hazael remind us of the words of Elijah and Elisha? (See 1 Kings 19:16-17 and 2 Kings 8:11-12.)

8. Why are the 'achievements' of Jehu (vv. 35-36) passed over in silence?

Questions to help apply the passage

1. How sincere do you think Jehu is in using the language of piety (v. 10)? Is there a danger for us of using spiritual-sounding language to disguise our real motives?

2. The mention of Judah (vv. 12-14) reminds us of the danger of compromising with God's enemies. Are there parallels in the lives of our churches?

3. The incident with Jehonadab (vv. 15-16) shows both Jehu's cunning and perhaps an all too ready acceptance by Jehonadab that reforming zeal is the same as true spiritual life. What can we learn from this about the danger of fanaticism?

4. Jehu destroyed Baal-worship but left generations of home grown idolatry untouched. Can we think of ways in which we can lapse into that attitude?

5. What does verse 34 tell us about the Lord's final assessment of the significance of what we have done?

10

THE BOY WONDER WHO CAME TO NOTHING (11 & 12)

Introduction

The dynastic purge is almost complete, except for Athaliah, daughter of Ahab and wife of Jehoram, former king of Judah (8:16-23), who launches a murderous attack to destroy what remains of the royal house of Judah. Much of that house had already been killed (10:12-14; 2 Chron. 22:10) but now she tries to destroy those who remain, presumably to salvage something for Ahab's house. As Queen Mother she now wants to seize power in her own right. The house of David has never looked more fragile.

This is the first main emphasis in these chapters: will the covenant promises to David (2 Sam. 7:16; Ps. 89:36) be fulfilled or will it go the same way as the house of Ahab? This is the reason why the narrative now returns to Judah, which, apart from a few brief mentions, has been very much in the background since 1 Kings 15. The chapters since then have largely focussed on Israel which is the setting for the great prophetic ministries of Elijah

and Elisha, along with other faithful men such as Micaiah
(1 Kings 22). God had promised Jeroboam back in 1 Kings
12:37-39 that He would raise up a parallel dynasty in the
north if His laws were obeyed. Jeroboam and his successors
spectacularly failed to do so. Yet the prophetic ministry left
them without excuse, prolonged as it was for half a century.

Here we are to be introduced to Joash, the surviving
member of David's house who initially looks promising
but goes off the rails. He is a 'yes but' king and the line of
David looks in as great peril at the end of his life as it did
at the beginning. As always, we need to remember that this
is God's story about God who is working His purpose out
in spite of His fierce enemies and often wavering friends.

Listening to the text

Context and structure

The origins of this crisis go back a generation to the reign of
Jehoshaphat, King of Judah. In 1 Kings 22:44 we are told
that he 'was at peace with the king of Israel'. This alliance
was cemented when his son Jehoram married Athaliah
(2 Kings 8:18). Both Jehoram and his son Ahaziah were
hopelessly compromised and 8:27 comments that Ahaziah
did evil because 'he was related by marriage to Ahab's
family'. See further comments on Jehoshaphat in *Teaching
1 Kings* pp. 31, 304 and 308. The consequences of a good
man's compromise nearly lead to total disaster.

Taking chapters 11 and 12 as a continuous story seven
acts unfold.

+   A vicious plot (11:1-3)

+   A successful coup (11:4-12)

+ The death of an oppressor (11:13-17)

+ A renewal of covenant (11:17-21)

+ An ambiguous start (12:1-3)

+ An obsession with money and fabric (12:4-16)

+ A bad ending (12:17-21)

Working through the text

A vicious plot (11:1-3)

The story here must be seen in its whole Biblical context where ultimately it is an attempt by the Serpent to destroy the descendant of the woman (Gen. 3:15). It is one of many such attempts: Pharaoh (Exod. 1); Haman (Esther 3-5); Herod (Matt. 2). Like these other and similar attempts, it appeared at first to be successful. Athaliah is not here called 'queen', nor is there the usual introductory statement about the occupant of the throne, because she is clearly regarded as a usurper.

The fightback at first seems low key and unlikely to have much effect. The sister of the late king Jehoram, Athaliah's daughter-in-law, sets out to frustrate the Queen Mother's wicked intentions. Jehosheba is one of the great unsung heroines of the Bible, in R. Davis' delightful phrase 'the lady who saved Christmas'.[1] On a human level the risk was enormous. Think of trying to keep a small boy hidden for six years![2]

---

1. Davis, *2 Kings* p. 167.

2. It is possible that he may not have been recognised by anyone other than his guardians, rather than that no one saw him. See Provan p. 219.

In any case the line of David is in a precarious state and embodied in a child who would have no least idea what was happening. Another one who had no least idea of what was happening was Athaliah herself and that was to prove her undoing.

A successful coup (11:4-12)

A new character now appears; this is Jehoiada, who is called priest in verses 9 and 15. He is almost certainly the high priest and we learn in 2 Chronicles 22:11 that he was Jehosheba's husband. Seven years into Athaliah's reign was long enough for people to see what she was like. Jehoiada is no hothead and he lays his plans carefully, sending for the 'commanders', probably of the royal guard, perhaps some of whom had been privy to the identity of the child. The Carites were probably desendants of the Kerethites who had been part of David's bodyguard (2 Sam. 20:23). Jehoiada swore them to secrecy as he outlined the plan to remove Athaliah and put Joash on throne.

His instructions in verses 5-8 are that on the appointed day the duty guards were subdivided into three: one third guarding the palace; one third at the surgate; and another third at an unidentified gate 'behind the guard'. The remaining two thirds, who would normally be off duty, were to guard Joash, already here named as the king (vv. 7-8). These instructions are followed and the emphasis on the weapons which had belonged to David (v.10) reminds us that it is the fate of the royal house which is at stake.

There follows a brief account of the crowning of Joash (v.12) and the presenting to him of 'a copy of the covenant'. This follows Deuteronomy 17:18-20 where the king is to receive this document which is to guide his personal and political life. It is these words which David urges Solomon to follow (1 Kings 2:2-4).

The death of an oppressor (11:13-17)
The willingness of the guards to follow Jehoiada and the enthusiasm with which the people receive Joash spells the end for Athaliah. The boy king was standing beside the pillar, probably Jakin or Boaz (see 1 Kings 7:21 and comments in *Teaching 1 Kings, p. 110*). Given what Athaliah had done to the royal princes her cry of 'treason' is rather hollow. Athaliah's end has come and she is removed from the temple and executed. So ends yet another 'Jezebel' who had defied Yahweh.

But her legacy remains to be destroyed. The covenant is not only about faithfulness to Yahweh but the removal of false gods. During Athaliah's regime, Baal-worship had flourished in Jerusalem and the temple to that god, so associated with Ahab's family, had to be destroyed and its priest removed.

A renewal of covenant (11:17-21)
This kind of covenant renewal ceremony happened with David (2 Sam. 5:3; 7:8-16) and was to happen later with Josiah (2 Kings 23:3). King and people pledged themselves to be faithful to God and follow His words. They had made a start by getting rid of Baal-worship and now positively needed to turn back to Yahweh.

Opposition for the moment has gone with the death of Athaliah, an event which had been greeted with rejoicing (v. 14). We are reminded that Joash is still a small boy and thus will need guidance and mentoring for many years to come. At the moment there is peace and the opportunity for a new start.

An ambiguous start (12:1-3)
At first, this new start seems promising. It is a long time
since the author has said that a king 'did what was right in
the eyes of the LORD' (12:2). And a forty-year reign raises
the possibility of a time of stability. However, there are
two qualifications to this favourable verdict. The first is
that the godly behaviour was confined to 'all the years that
Jehoiada the priest instructed him'. The priest would have
gained considerable respect for his coup against Athaliah
and indeed he was eventually to be buried among the kings
(2 Chron. 24:16-27). There is the suggestion that there was
something second hand about Joash's faith which did not
survive the period of mentoring. The second is that the
'high places' with all their temptation to the wrong kind
of worship remained (12:3). At this point the king is young
and still learning and the story could go either way.

An obsession with money and fabric (12:4-16)
Once again here is a promising beginning. Solomon's
temple was now over a hundred years' old and had almost
certainly been neglected by Jehoram and Ahaziah. Very
probably Athaliah had pillaged it to furnish Baal's temple.
So turning attention to repair the temple was laudable.
However, as we reflect on the story it makes for dull and
dispiriting reading. What is striking is what is not in it.
There is nothing said about the Word of God or about
prayer; this is simply a job to be done. Neither priests nor
king come out of it well.

The priests appeared more concerned about their own
pockets than the use of funds for temple repair. This does
not necessarily mean that they were dishonest but that they
were not wholly committed to the work. What about the

role of Jehoiada in all this? We learn that he made a money box and that he would supervise the disbursing of funds for the repair of the temple when it became full. We also need to remember that by this time, twenty-three years into Joash's reign, Jehoiada would be becoming old. The account in 2 Chronicles 24 says he died at the advanced age of a hundred and thirty and implies that this was not too long after the events surrounding the repair of the temple. The overall impression is that the priest's concern was with money and fabric, especially as their regular income was untouched (v. 16).

But what of the king? Admittedly he was only seven when he was crowned and presumably it was some time after that that he gave instructions for the repairs on the temple to begin. However, waiting until he had been twenty-three years on the throne when he was thirty seems to hint at lack of enthusiasm on his own part. Also, in contrast to the building of the temple, there is no heartfelt prayer, unlike 1 Kings 8:22-53, nor any national celebration (1 Kings 8:62-66). We shall see a similar contrast when Josiah undertakes temple repairs (2 Kings 22-23). There is no sense here of the presence of God and no trembling at His Word.

A bad ending (12:17-21)

The story of the boy wonder who came to nothing limps to its disappointing ending. Joash fails to provide military leadership. Hazael, king of Syria, who had attacked Israel at the end of Jehu's reign now turns his attention to Judah and the future of David's throne is again in doubt. Joash attempts to buy off this threat by plundering the very temple treasury that he had earlier attempted to build up.

The reign is to end in disaster with the assassination of the king who had been crowned with such bright hopes forty years before. Probably that was at least partly due to disaffection following his failure to deal decisively with Syria. However, the parallel account in 2 Chronicles 24:17-27 paints a darker picture of Joash's apostasy and turning to idolatry which culminates in the murder of Zechariah[3], son of Jehoiada who had condemned him. Here the emphasis is more on the crushing disappointment of the king who had promised so much and delivered so little.

It is here that we need to have a firm grasp of the big picture as the line of David again seems to be in mortal danger. Joash was not that promised Son of David who would bring in the kingdom which would never end. But that king would come and neither the rage of His enemies here represented by Athaliah, nor the failure of fair weather friends such as Joash could prevent this.

From text to message

Getting the message clear: the theme

God's kingdom is always in danger whether from the attacks of its enemies or the failure of its friends. Few stories are as disappointing as this one and it is a mercy that Jehosheba and Jehoiada were no longer alive to see the dashing of their hopes.

Getting the message clear: the aim

We need to be warned that temporary triumphs do not mean that the kingdom has come already or we will be

---

3.   This is the Zechariah mentioned by Jesus in Matthew 23:35 as one of the noble army of martyred prophets who had been rejected by the establishment.

doomed to disappointment. However, we need to keep our eyes fixed on the King who will not disappoint and who will fulfil all His promises.

A way in

Perhaps it would be good to examine what we really expect the Lord to do and whether we are too excited by temporary successes and too downcast by temporary failures. Rudyard Kipling's once famous poem *If* contains the lines:

> *If you can meet with triumph and disaster,*
> *And treat these two imposters just the same.*

Kipling did not mean that triumph and disaster did not happen, but they were 'imposters' in the sense that neither was the full reality. So here neither the viciousness of Athaliah, nor the bitter disappointment of Joash was the full picture of what was happening; rather both of these were caught up in the purposes of God as He prepared to send His Son.

Ideas for application

+ Sometimes in a crisis the response of the Lord seems low key and inadequate; here a baby boy hidden in a bedroom. But so often this leads to greater things: baby Moses in Exodus 2 and most notably the baby who is the Saviour of the world.

+ God's work does not set aside careful planning; Jehoiada's coup was very cleverly and systematically organised.

+ We need to have a faith which will still be alive when our mentors are no longer there.

+ None of our church buildings whether magnificent cathedrals or Nissen huts correspond to the temple (see exposition of 1 Kings 8) but we can learn important principles. Here, even if the repair of what was God's dwelling place among His people was simply treated as the repair of a building and it had no impact on the spiritual life of king, priests and people, how much more does this apply to our building projects?

+ When prayer and the Word of God are not central, spiritual life dies and organised religion takes its place.

+ Beginning well does not guarantee continuing and finishing well.

+ In case the last point leads to feelings of despair, God's work continues, there is a new son of David, Amaziah, on the throne and the Son of David who is to come will give us grace to help in time of need.

Suggestions for preaching

This is a long section but it has strong narrative unity. Suggestions will be made for preaching on both chapters as a whole as well as separately.

Sermon 1

This would concentrate on the dangers facing the kingdom of God and its eventual triumph.

God's kingdom cannot fail

+ The preserving of the son of David.

God's kingdom is based on covenant

✦ Both king and people need to be faithful to God and His Word.

God's kingdom needs heart commitment not just formalities

✦ The disappointment of this son of David.

Sermon 2
This focusses on chapter 11 and on God's judgment on His enemies.

A plot which failed

✦ God's enemies cannot ultimately succeed.

A necessary purge

✦ Both civil and religious idolatry need to be removed.

A renewal of covenant

✦ Recalling nation to its roots.

Sermon 3
This concentrates on chapter 12 and the unfulfilled potential of the boy wonder who came to nothing.

Don't rely on someone else's faith

✦ Qualified commendation of Joash.

Don't overemphasise money and fabric

✦ Lack of Word of God and prayer.

Don't become complacent in later life

✦ Total disappointment and temple reforms undone.

Suggestions for teaching

Questions to help understand the passage

1. Why does Athaliah want to destroy the family of David and why does she almost succeed?

2. How do we know that Jehosheba was not only brave but resourceful?

3. What do we learn about how Jehoiada is respected by the royal bodyguard?

4. How do we know that he was a careful planner as well as a man of faith?

5. What does the mention of King David and the temple of the LORD (11:10) tell us about Jehoiada's motivation?

6. How do we know that Athaliah did not have the loyalty of the people?

7. Why is the destruction of Baal's temple mentioned?

8. In what ways is Joash's faith shown to be unsatisfactory?

9. What is missing in the account of the temple repairs?

10. What does the phrase 'the other events of the reign of Joash and all that he did' (12:19) suggest about the writer's final assessment of Joash?

Questions to help apply the passage

1. How does compromise in one generation lead to disaster in the next? (It would be useful to read

again 1 Kings 22 about Jehoshaphat's ill-advised liaison with the house of Ahab.)

2. What does Jehosheba's action show us about the importance of otherwise unknown people in the kingdom of God?

3. Jehoiada is very conscious that what he is doing is not just about regime change. In what ways can we learn from his emphasis on the covenant?

4. Baalism needed to be destroyed for the covenant to be re-established? What kind of things need to be got rid of for truly biblical patterns to be established?

5. We all need mentors and godly examples but how do we guard against becoming over-dependent on them?

6. What is missing in this building project and how do we avoid a similar mistake?

7. We need to avoid beginning well and ending badly. How can we guard against this?

11

THE END OF AN ERA (13)

Introduction

After the violence of the last few chapters we appear to be entering a time of comparative peace between Israel and Judah (although that is by no means stable as we shall see in 14:8-14). War with Syria continues as had been predicted and the significance of this will be examined. In this world God's people will never enjoy total peace although there are times of respite. The chapter describes the reigns of two kings of Israel, Jehoash[1] and Jehoahaz. The timescale is from approximately 814 to 781 B.C. The story of the two kings shows the mixture of sin and grace characteristic of the whole narrative and the chapter ends with the affirming of God's covenant faithfulness.

Yet far more significant is the main focus of the chapter which is the close of Elisha's great ministry which had lasted for more than sixty years. In the Introduction (pp. 30-1) the

---

1. Also, like his Judaean counterpart can be called Joash. To avoid confusion I follow NIV in referring to the Israelite king as Jehoash.

long central section running from 1 Kings 17 to 2 Kings 13 was seen to be dominated by the great prophetic ministries of Elijah and Elisha and their involvement in the life of the northern kingdom. It is this emphasis on the passing of Elisha and his continuing influence which gives us our bearings and shows that these ministries were far more important than the kings to whom they spoke. Others would soon take up the torch: Hosea and Amos in the north, followed later by Micah and Isaiah in the south. Yet this is the end of an era and the voice which had spoken so powerfully for over half a century was to be heard no more, but significantly its influence was to continue.

Listening to the text

Context and structure.

The immediate context is Yahweh's promise to Jehu that his descendants would reign in the north for four generations (10:30) and here the first two of these emerge (the end of the dynasty is described in 15:8-12). Neither are godly but both turn to Yahweh at times of crisis. The background to both reigns is war with Syria which had been a recurring motif since the reign of Ahab (1 Kings 20, 22) and had often been a way in which God had punished His people (see esp. 2 Kings 5:1). The significance of the end of Elisha's ministry has already been noted. The story develops in five acts:

+ Sin and grace (13:1-9)

+ An insignificant reign (13:10-13)

+ Elisha finishes the race (13:14-19)

+ Speaking still although dead (13:20-21)

+ Covenant faithfulness (13:22-25)

Working through the text

Sin and grace (13:1-9)

Jehu's reform and purge of Baalism had not turned the north back to Yahweh. The Jeroboam cult is alive and well and the suggestion is that this was no mere lapse on the part of Jehoahaz', he did not turn away'. This had consequences in military terms both under Hazael of Syria who had already oppressed Israel (8:12; 10:32-3) and continued under his son Ben-Hadad. God is Lord of history and later prophets develop the theme that God will use powerful nations to punish His own people for disobedience. Isaiah is to say that about the Assyrians (Isa. 10:5-18) and Habakkuk about the Babylonians (Hab. 1:5-11)

But if this is a story about sin it is also a story about grace and when Jehoahaz prays, God hears and answers. It is important to realise that none of our prayers would be answered without grace because even at our most sincere we have mixed motives. Rather than wondering about why God answered this man's prayer we need to see that this is an insight into the kind of God to whom we pray. There is a deliberate echo of the Exodus story. Just as God listened to the groaning of His people in slavery in Egypt (Exod. 2:24;3:7) He now sees the oppression of Syria and feels the same concern. God and not Jeroboam's calf idols (1 Kings 12:28) had brought them out of slavery and He is the same God who sends a deliverer, a saviour.[2]

---

2. Commentators differ about the identity of this deliverer. Some see it as a reference to the defeats of Syria by later kings such as Jehoash and Jeroboam. This is unlikely because the text implies that the rescue came in Jehoahaz' reign. Perhaps more likely is that this refers to a resurgent Assyria under Adad-nirari III who began to threaten Syria and caused them to withdraw from Israel.

However, more important than identifying the precise saviour here is seeing the Gospel light shining. The God of our salvation is to come Himself in the person of His Son and while we were still enemies rescue us from the slavery of sin. In this obscure narrative in a little-read part of Scripture, Christ is seen and we are reminded that failure and sin can only be covered by grace.

It is grace indeed but grace that was rejected once the danger was past (v. 6). The prayer was answered but idolatry continued unchecked and Jeroboam's idols were again embraced as if they had been the saviours. The Asherah pole which Ahab had set up in Samaria (1 Kings 16:33) and not mentioned as having been removed by Jehu still drew people's hearts away from Yahweh. This remains a danger. It leads to prayer being seen as wanting solutions to problems rather than a developing relationship with the Lord.

In any case Jehoahaz' army was in a sorry state and the king's 'achievements' such as they were are condemned to oblivion in lost annals. The king's reputation has proved as insubstantial as his army and crumbled into dust.

An insignificant reign (13:10-13)

We are not reassured by the brief notice of his son Jehoash; indeed little more is said than that he reigned, sinned and died (see also 14:9-16). The war with Amaziah of Judah is listed as one of his achievements but that is developed in chapter 14. What are we to make of this short account?

Two things can be said. The first is that we are being shown how Yahweh is continuing to fulfil His promise about Jehu's descendants. Nothing was said about the quality of his heirs, simply that his dynasty would continue.

But second, and more important, his reign is the backdrop to the finishing of Elisha's ministry. This both marginalises Jehoash and also gives him the opportunity to return to Yahweh and reject the ways of Jeroboam.

Elisha finishes the race (13:14-19)

No details are given of Elisha's illness nor of the location, although we know from chapter 5 that he had a house in Samaria. Just as Jehoahaz had turned to Yahweh in a time of crisis, now Jehoash realises that Elisha will soon be gone and fears for the future. Indeed he echoes the words of Elisha himself in 2:12 when Elijah was taken to heaven, 'my father.. the chariots and horsemen of Israel', grimly appropriate here in view of what had happened to the chariots of Israel (v. 7). Was he being sincere or was he simply being deferential to the old prophet who had been so influential both in national politics and individual lives? We do not know and in any case he speaks more wisely than he knows as the prophet and Elijah before him had indeed been a bulwark for the nation.

It is the dying prophet who is in charge and gives orders to the king in a striking visual aid, ordering him to shoot arrows out of the east window. Elisha holds the bow along with Jehoash and explains that the arrow is a sign of victory (lit. salvation, carrying on the theme of v. 5) over Syria. The point is how enthusiastically will the king obey? To Elisha's dismay the king is satisfied with three shots, far from the complete destruction he had predicted in verse 17. This was half-hearted faith. The phrase 'and stopped' suggests a deliberate action and possibly his feeling that he had already done enough to humour the old man. The obedience of Jehoash has self-imposed limits and is far from the faith which would have seen an end to the Syrian threat.

Speaking still although dead (13:20-21)

Elisha is dead and buried and it would be too easy to think of his ministry as a failure. After all, the nation remained godless and while Baalism had been removed the idolatry of Jeroboam continued unchecked. We have seen how God authenticated Elijah's ministry by taking him to heaven and now this odd little episode shows him authenticating Elisha's ministry. Some Israelites are burying a man, and surprised by Moabite raiders they throw his body into Elisha's tomb and when the man comes into contact with Elisha's bones he comes to life.

Some have seen this as superstitious magic and dismissed it as a bizarre relic from a credulous age. Others, wanting to salvage something, see it as a symbolic narrative of God throwing Israel into exile and then bringing them back to life. The point is that indeed there is symbolism (as in the valley of dry bones in Ezekiel 37) but a story can be factually true as well as symbolic. Indeed, that is a characteristic of Biblical narrative: events true in themselves happening to people who actually lived but also giving insight into a deeper reality of God's overall purpose.

If an important theme in this chapter is about salvation, then indeed we can see how Elisha's ministry, so effective in his lifetime in bringing life out of death, is authenticated by that same power which operated during his earthly ministry. More than that, it points to the day when death itself will be destroyed. Perhaps the passage most similar to this is Matthew 27:51-3 where the tombs are opened at Jesus' death and some bodies of the saints come out after

His resurrection. That passage like this one is strange but the basic meaning is clear that the day is coming when all who are in the grave will hear the voice of the Son of God and come out (John 5:27). Thus Elisha, although dead, still speaks (Heb. 11:4).

Covenant faithfulness (13:22-25)
This little section forms a bridge between the long section on Elijah and Elisha and the next section outlining the gradual slip to Exile for the southern kingdom, and the deportation of the northern kingdom to Assyria. It begins with a reminder of Syrian oppression but majors on God's covenant faithfulness. We know there is a future for Judah because of the covenant with David but there is no such assurance for Israel. Here we are reminded of that earlier covenant with Abraham, Isaac and Jacob which envisaged not two but one nation which would be re-united and blessed (see e.g. Ezek. 37:15-28). From the valley of dry bones new life will emerge. Remember that this book ends with Israel already gone and Judah in Babylon but the covenant faithfulness of God will bring them back.

In the immediate context verse 24 shows the fulfilment of Elisha's dying prophecy; victories but limited ones because of Jehoash's lack of faith. God still speaks to His people and will continue to speak up to the brink of Exile, during it and beyond it. The covenant is unbreakable from God's side but for His people to enjoy its blessings there needs to be repentance and faith.

From text to message

Getting the message clear: the theme
The main theme is that the prophetic ministry is more significant and lasting than the kings who happen to be in power. Elisha's earthly life and ministry come to an end but its effect remains. The words of Isaiah 40:8, 'The grass withers and the flowers fall, but the Word of our God stands for ever' are relevant here. The context in Isaiah shows that the grass and flowers are the kingdoms of the world.

Getting the message clear: the aim
God's faithfulness shown not least in the ministry of His prophets remains constant but there needs to be obedience. Jehoash failed to give wholehearted obedience and the consequences were evident, yet God's covenant Word was not broken.

A way in
How do we assess the effectiveness of a work of God? Here the ministry of Elisha, like that of Elijah, in spite of many triumphs has not turned the nation back to God. Yet in both cases, although in very different ways, the Lord authenticates the ministry of His servants. We need to emphasise that only the Lord will give the final assessment on all work for Him.

Ideas for application
*   God's saving hand is to be found everywhere in the story, not just in the effective Davidic kings but in the fact that everywhere (like the unnamed saviour of v. 4) He is preparing the way for His kingdom. Even if that

saviour is an Assyrian king that is no more surprising than calling Cyrus, the Lord's anointed (Isa. 45:1).

+ God vindicates His faithful servants; if not on earth then in eternity.

+ Prayer is not primarily about the removing of problems but about a renewed relationship with the Lord.

+ The covenant Lord remains faithful; this is not an excuse for sin but a call to renewed commitment.

Suggestions for preaching

Sermon 1
This follows the flow of the story with two major points and one which is a footnote, albeit an important one.

The king sins but grace abounds (13:1-7)
Sin has consequences in every part of life (here Jehoahaz' military disasters are a consequence of his idolatry). Yet his prayer, although far from fully sincere, was answered.

The king dies but the prophet lives (13:10-21)
What Jehoash did was of little consequence but Elisha's work was of eternal significance.

The covenant cannot be broken (13:22-25)
Covenant binds the story together and God's ancient promises stand.

Sermon 2
This looks at the contrasting personalities.

Two ineffective kings
The link of idolatry and failure in all aspects of life.

An effective prophet
Elisha's continuing ministry.

Suggestions for teaching

Questions to help understand the passage

1. What evidence is there that Jehoahaz sinned deliberately? (See v. 2.)

2. Why did the Lord listen to Jehoahaz?

3. How do we know that Jehoash was ineffective? (v. 12)

4. What is the point of the incident of striking the arrow?

5. How do we know that Jehoash's obedience was partial? (See v. 18.)

6. What does the incident involving Elisha's bones tell us about the continuing power of his ministry?

7. Why is Jehoahaz introduced again in verse 22?

8. Why is the covenant with the patriarchs mentioned here?

9. How does verse 25 show the truth of Elisha's last words?

Questions to help apply the passage

1. What do we learn about how God deals with sin in verses 1-3?

2. In what ways do our prayers often show that we want relief rather than transformation?

3. What is verse 12 implying about 'achievements' which are accomplished by merely human means?

4. In what ways does this chapter show the effectiveness of the prophet's Word; indeed, its continuing effectiveness even today?

5. How does the episode in verse 21 teach us not to underestimate God?

6. What is the relationship of the unconditional covenant and human obedience?

12

KINGS COME AND GO (14 & 15)

Introduction

At first sight these chapters (especially 15) seem rather meagre fare with brief notes on kings who come and go and appear to make little impact. The time scale is approximately sixty years from 796 to 732 B.C. and the temptation is to rush over this section. However, there are important underlying currents which give us our bearings and continue the big story. Three points can be made.

First the promises of Yahweh to both Judah and Israel are underlined. In Judah the Davidic line continues unbroken. In Israel the promise that Jehu's line would last four generations (2 Kings 10:30) is fulfilled in 15:12. This is a reminder that whatever the conditions and failures, God is faithful. This is something we need to remember as still true in our day. The Word of God still shapes events. There is the mention of Jonah (14:25) and, as we shall see, the beginning of other prophetic ministries.

Second, there is mercy as well as judgment. In the reign of Jeroboam II (14:23-9), God's compassion gives to the northern kingdom forty years of peace and prosperity. Similarly, the failures of the kings of Judah does not set aside the covenant with David. In Judah the three kings mentioned: Amaziah, Azariah (Uzziah) and Jotham all receive genuine, if qualified, praise. In Israel the kings are universally idolatrous but Jeroboam is still used by God.

Third, the shadow of Assyria begins to fall over the story and the possibility of exile looms larger. This had been anticipated in Solomon's prayer (1 Kings 8:46ff) and now the possibility is drawing nearer. This is to be fulfilled first in the exile of Israel to Assyria and then the exile of Judah to Babylon.

Listening to the text

Context and Structure

The great prophetic ministries of Elijah and Elisha are over, but the Word of God remains and the mention of Jonah underlines this. There is also an increasing sense of events, especially in the northern kingdom moving in a downward spiral and the ominous threat from Assyria grows.

We shall look at the story in five stages:

+ God does not settle for second best (14:1-22)

+ God's grace in spite of sin (14:23-29)

+ A wasted opportunity (15:1-7)

+ Plunging to destruction (15:8-31)

+ Judah still on track (15:32-8)

Working through the text

God does not settle for second best (14:1-22)
We are introduced to the first of the kings of Judah whom we might call the 'yes but' kings who are relatively good but lack wholehearted commitment. Indeed, that is made specific in the account of Amaziah's reign in 2 Chronicles, 'He did what was right in the eyes of the LORD, yet not wholeheartedly' (2 Chron. 25:2). Here he is specifically contrasted with David and said to follow the rather uninspiring example of his father Joash (v. 3). But God does not want another Joash, He wants another David. Also his reign is overshadowed by Jehoash of Israel who dominates verses 8-14. Here is a king who has settled for second best. This is shown in a number of ways. The notorious high places are not removed and indeed we are going to have to wait for Hezekiah in chapter 18 before this problem is dealt with. He does indeed obey Deuteronomy 24:16 by not killing the sons of the assassins of his father. The trouble is that Amaziah's obedience to the Torah is selective. Numbers 33:52 commands the destruction of the high places. Often today we have a pick and mix attitude to the Bible, choosing those parts which suit us. God's truth is one truth.

Another part of his story shows us that God's judgments are always at work, we have often seen this as we have looked at the history. Sometimes God gives victory as He does against Edom (v. 7). Other times He sends defeat. It is not clear why Amaziah decided to challenge Jehoash (v. 8). Indeed, it sounds rather like a macho boast which wants confrontation rather than conference: 'meet me face to face,' has the same nuance as the contemporary expression

'in your face'. Unfortunately for Amaziah, Jehoash is
good with words as well as in battle and he mocks the
pretensions of the king of Judah: 'you're no cedar, you're
a thistle' and shows up the arrogance of Amaziah (v. 10).
The king is captured, parts of Jerusalem are destroyed and
the temple is ransacked. It is not clear how long Amaziah
was in Samaria; perhaps he was released immediately or
by Jeroboam. In any case it is a sorry tale of pride and
boasting leading to humiliation. Indeed, Amaziah not only
follows Joash in his life but suffers the same kind of death
by assassination.

Yet it is not all gloom. The Davidic line continues with
Azariah and the apparently irrelevant detail that he 'rebuilt
Elath and restored it to Judah' (v. 22). But Elath was a very
important centre of international trade at the time and we
are reminded that one day a son of David will reign over
the whole world.

God's grace in spite of sin (14:29)
We return to Israel and to one of the most effective of all
its kings, Jeroboam who reigned from 793-753 B.C. He is
usually known as Jeroboam II to distinguish him from
Israel's first king, 'Jeroboam, son of Nebat,' who led Israel
into sin (14:24; 15:9, 18, 28). This was Israel's last period of
peace and prosperity and contrasts sharply with the brief
reigns which followed. This coincided with a relatively
weak regime in Assyria which left Jeroboam free to pursue
his policies home and abroad.[1] However there was a darker
side in the growing gap between rich and poor, reflected
especially by Amos who ministered during this time (see
esp. Amos 2:6-7; 4:1; 5:11-15; 6:1-7; 8:4-6). Amos confirms

---

1.   See Wiseman p 248.

the restoration of land in 6:13-14 but sees it as the root of dangerous complacency. The reference to Jonah (v. 25) reminds us of the backdrop of prophetic activity even when it is not described in the text.

Yet the events of this prosperous reign which stretched over four decades are dealt with in a summary manner. The real importance of this time is what is said in verses 26-7. Yahweh still loves His straying people and cares for them and gives them a time of relative stability when they can return to Him. We need not be surprised that Jeroboam is seen as a saviour; in 13:5 the saviour may be the king of Assyria and later Cyrus is to be seen in that role (Isa. 45:1). Israel will go into exile, as will Judah, but the prophets look to the day of the united people of God entering their inheritance (e.g. Ezek. 37:15-19). When that happens it will be under the rule of David (Ezek. 37:24-8) and that will be the reign of peace and harmony when David's greater Son will gather the nations.

The promise to Jehu (2 Kings 10:30) is fulfilled in the accession of Jeroboam's son Zechariah (v. 29), another reminder that Assyrian weakness, Jeroboam's firm rule and other factors are secondary causes because it is Yahweh who rules in the kingdoms of men. The growth of territory was a gift of God.

A wasted opportunity (15:1-7)
A few brief verses outline the fifty-two year reign of Azariah, better known as Uzziah.[2] The much fuller account in 2 Chronicles 26 shows him as a strong king, like David

---

2.   It is probable that he was co-regent with his father Amaziah after Amaziah's ill-fated war with Jehoash of Israel and later Jotham was co-regent with him. See Wiseman p 250.

in his military conquests and Solomon in his building and
care for the land. Yet all this turns to ashes with the chilling
phrase 'he was greatly helped until he became powerful'
and he was struck with a debilitating skin disease which
prevented him carrying out his royal duties.[3] His reign
was longer than the five Israelite kings of the next verses
combined and that again is a sign of Yahweh's mercy. It
was a reign which began with much promise but the great
opportunities were squandered.

Here is another 'yes but' king who follows his father
rather than David and again there is failure to remove
the high places. The 'other events' (v. 6) are outlined in
2 Chronicles 26 and show him like Jeroboam in Israel
recovering territory. It was in the year of his death that
Isaiah had his vision of the Lord (Isa. 6:1).

Plunging to destruction (15:8-31)

By contrast with the long reign of Azariah and indeed
Jeroboam II, Israel is plunged into a time of chaos and
coups. Yet in all this we are reminded that the Word of
Yahweh is directing events (v. 12). We are also reminded
that the kings of Israel seem to have learned nothing in their
following of the sins of the first Jeroboam (vv. 9, 18, 28).

With Zechariah's six month reign the line of Jehu
comes to an end (v. 12). Shallum, an otherwise unknown
figure, is used to fulfil the prophecy of 2 Kings 10:30. As
often noticed before that does not mean Yahweh approved
of Shallum or his action, any more than other violent acts
but that He uses these to work out His purpose. In any

---

3.   The phrase 'a separate house' (v. 5) probably means he lived, probably
      in considerable comfort, in a house away from the administrative
      centre where Jotham exercised the royal duties as regent.

case the hapless Shallum lasts a mere month when he is assassinated by Menahem who may have been an army commander at Tirzah, capital of the country before Omri founded Samaria (1 Kings 16:23-4).

Menahem's reign was longer, ten years in fact, but they were grim years. The first thing noted was his merciless cruelty (v. 16). Tiphsah's location is unknown but the atrocity towards pregnant women and their unborn children is unparalleled by any other Israelite king and a shocking disregard for God's law. To this sadism he added idolatry and never deviated from the path to ruin (v. 18).

The next significant event is the rise of Assyria now bent on world conquest. Pul was the personal name of Tiglath Pileser III (v. 19) and this is the beginning of the process which is to result in the deportation of Israel and a massive threat to Judah. Menahem bought him off by paying a huge indemnity which he raised by harsh means. The word 'exacted' (v. 20) reveals yet another facet of the unscrupulousness of this man, surely one of the most unpleasant characters in the story. Probably fear that the Assyrians would return was a further motive to pay these large sums. Indeed, he is the only one of the kings here who manages a 'dynasty', if indeed that is an appropriate name for one successor.

That successor is his son Pekahiah about whose brief two-year reign we know only that he was a follower of Jeroboam son of Nebat. Surely the reference to the 'fiftieth year of Azariah' is a reminder that in spite of that king's faults he carried on the Davidic line, in stark contrast to the fleeting reigns in the North not undergirded by divine promise. Pekahiah suffers the fate of assassination at the hands of Pekah, one of his army officers. It is not clear

whether Argob and Arieh (v. 25) are personal names or
place names but that is a minor detail. Yet another usurper
sits on the throne of Israel.

Pekah's reign lasts twenty years which might seem to
offer a time of stability but this was not to be. Now the
Assyrian menace looms ever larger. If Menahem had
bought off Assyria and his son Pekahiah had followed that
policy, it seems likely that Pekah had wanted to distance
himself from them and thus adopt an anti-Assyrian stance
which brought the unwelcome attention of Tiglath-Pileser.
The Assyrian king takes much of northern Israel and
deports the people; the final exile of the kingdom is near.

Pekah also suffers the fate of assassination at the hands
of Hoshea whose name ironically means 'saviour'. He is
to be the last king of Israel but we do not yet know that.
Tiglath-Pileser's annals show that he installed Hoshea as
a puppet king.[4]

Judah is still on track (15:32-8)
The section ends, as it began, with a king of Judah, Jotham
who reigned for sixteen years. Jotham had already been co-
regent for a number of years when his father Uzziah was
disabled. The now familiar qualified approval that the king
followed his father rather than David and that he did not
remove the high places occurs again. Yet the main point is
that while Israel plunges to ruin, the Davidic line continues.

The account is sketchy and does not mention Jotham's
victory over the Ammonites (2 Chron. 27:5). It does,
however, tell of his rebuilding of the Upper Gate of
the temple (v. 35). It was in his reign that Micah began
his ministry (Micah 1:1) and he is one of the four kings

---

4.   Wiseman p257.

mentioned in the backdrop to Isaiah's ministry (Isa. 1:1). The Word of God is active during Jotham's reign.

The renewed hostility of Syria, this time allied with Israel, begins here (v. 37) but the full consequences of this are only worked out in Ahaz' reign (16:5-9). The kingdom of Judah has still not gone the way of Israel, but all is not well, and the next chapter will show ominous developments.

From text to message

Getting the message clear: the theme:
The overall theme is that in the midst of human incompetence and worse, God's purposes will be carried out. His promises do not depend on the human instruments He uses and while from an earthly perspective all may seem chaotic He knows the end from the beginning.

Getting the message clear: the aim:
The aim is to encourage people to trust in the Lord of history who is not taken by surprise or thrown off track by events. This is the underlying message of much of OT history and is a lesson every generation needs to learn.

A way in
A former British Prime Minister, Harold Macmillan, was once asked what was the most difficult thing about his job. He replied, 'Events, dear boy, events'. This is a problem for lesser mortals as well as prime ministers. How do we make sense of the bewildering cataract of events on the world stage? At the time of writing the horrors of the war in Syria, the Islamic state, Russia flexing her muscles and global economic issues dominate the headlines. The decision of the U.K. to leave the European Union and the

uncertainty following the election of Mr Donald Trump as
the President of the U.S.A. create a sense of nervousness
and fear of an unknown future. All that is reproduced on a
smaller scale in our communal and personal lives.

This calls for faith in a God who is faithful and in
control and these chapters, far from being remote and
dull, present that challenge to a robust faith in the Lord
of History whose Son the true Davidic king will reign for
ever and ever.

Ideas for application

+ The faithfulness of God is not simply a doctrine, it is
  the only basis for faithful living in this world. The kings
  of Judah here all have good potential but achieve less
  than they might have because of fickle allegiance.

+ The story of Jeroboam II (14:23-9) is a reminder
  of God's common grace and His overall desire for
  humanity to be blessed.

+ Repeated sin grows worse over the generations. Here
  this is especially shown in the brutal reign of Menahem
  (15:17-22).

+ The Word of God never fails and this is encouragement
  to keep on preaching and teaching.

+ The Davidic line is flawed as was David himself but the
  Son who would not fail would come to reign.

Suggestions for preaching

There is probably too much material for one sermon. One
way to tackle it would be to do separate sermons on the
kings of Judah and the kings of Israel.

Sermon 1

David's sons: warts and all (14:1-22; 15:1-7;32-38)
Two matters: unfulfilled potential and God's faithfulness
to His covenant.

+ Qualified approval: following their fathers rather than
  David and failure to remove the high places.

+ Imperfect obedience to Torah (see esp. Amaziah).

+ Sense of fragility: Amaziah's weakness in face of
  Jehoash; Uzziah's leprosy; Jotham threatened by Syria
  and Israel.

But conclusion needs to emphasise God's covenant
faithfulness to David and His commitment to sending
David's greater Son.

Sermon 2

*Judgment inevitable: the doomed throne of Israel (14:23-9;
15:8-31)*

+ God's promises are still fulfilled: 15:12 keeping promise
  to Jehu in 10:30.

+ Prophetic voices: Jonah (14:25) and off-stage Amos.

  + Grace gives time to repent – the long and prosperous
    reign of Jeroboam II.

  + Repeated sin gets worse esp Menahem (15:17-22).

  + Growing chaos shows God already judging.

+ Israel is doomed but God still cares.

Suggestions for teaching

Questions to help understand the passage:

1. Why does Amaziah challenge Jehoash? (14:8)

2. Why is Jehoash's obituary here (14:15-16) when we have had it already in 13:12, 13?

3. How do we know Jeroboam II was a strong king? (14:25)

4. Why is Jonah mentioned? (14:25b)

5. What do 14:26-7 tell us about the nature of Yahweh?

6. Why did Azariah's long reign end in failure? (15:1-7)

7. What is the point of 15:12?

8. What do we learn of the evil consequences of repeated sin especially in the case of Menahem? (15:17-22)

9. What do 15:19 and 29 tell us about the changing world situation?

10. What kind of king was Jotham? (15:32-7)

Questions to help apply the passage:

1. What are the dangers of half-hearted commitment and partial obedience, looking particularly at the three kings of Judah?

2. Why does the Lord sometimes give victory and sometimes defeat? How is this related to obedience?

3. What does the reign of Jeroboam tell us about God's grace and providence?

4. What do we learn about unfulfilled potential, looking especially at 15:1-7?

5. How do these chapters continue the theme of the power of the Word of God?

6. Why is Menahem's violence emphasised (15:16)? Does this relate to the judgment of the Exile? Have a look at Genesis 6:11 about violence and the judgment of the Flood.

7. How do we make sense of God sending Assyria against His people? Read 2 Kings 5 again and study Isaiah 10:5-34.

13

NOT STANDING AT ALL (16)

Introduction

As so often in the story a change of tempo marks a change of emphasis. The previous chapter has been characterised by brief notes on seven kings but now a whole chapter is devoted to the next king of Judah.[1] As we have seen the northern kingdom is rushing towards the abyss while the kings of Judah have been moderately good. Is this new king in the South the one who will lead the nation in paths of godliness? We are rapidly disabused of that idea. While Amaziah, Azariah (Uzziah) and Jotham had been reasonably loyal to Yahweh, this new king Ahaz deliberately sets out to ape the kings of Israel. Loud alarm bells are sounding. Is Judah going to share in Israel's fate?

---

1. There are problems with chronology here. Ahaz was probably co-regent with Jotham from 735 B.C. and sole ruler after Jotham's death in 732 B.C. This does not affect our preaching of this and other passages but it is good to be reminded of the accuracy of the author. Those looking for an authoritative account of this and other chronological difficulties will find this in Wiseman pages 26-35.

The international scene is darkening with the growing power of Assyria (see historical note) under its able king Tiglath-Pileser. Israel will shortly fall to Assyria and Judah is to teeter on the brink of the same fate. This is related to how the king is going to react in a crisis. The first threat to Ahaz comes not from Assyria, but from a coalition between Israel and Syria. There is an account of this episode in Isaiah 7, where the prophet urges the king not to be afraid of the enemy but to have faith in God. This is summed up in the prophet's words, 'If you do not stand firm in faith, you will not stand at all' (Isa. 7:9). This chapter is about a king who did not stand at all because he did not stand firm in faith.

Listening to the text

Context and Structure

There is a sense of approaching doom in this chapter as Ahaz strays further and further from the path of covenant promises. This is no careless slide from the truth but a deliberate walking in godless ways. Instead of trusting Yahweh the king deliberately places himself under the protection of a pagan emperor.

The story unfolds in four scenes:

+   Deadly disobedience (16:1-4)

+   Dangerous alliance (16:5-9)

+   Disobedient religion (16:10-18)

+   Dawning of hope (16:19-20)

Working through the text

Deadly disobedience (16:1-4)

The assessment of this king contrasts him with David (v. 2) and thus shows him deliberately cutting himself off from the covenant promises. Ahaz' predecessors had not totally followed David, but had at least 'done right' if in a qualified way. Here is a new departure and the sins of Jeroboam are now seeping into the south. The irony is that Ahaz, who doubtless saw himself as a man of the world and an astute politician, was following Israel's lead at the very time it was about to disappear into the dustbin of history.

The text spells out briefly but cogently what walking in the ways of the kings of Israel meant (v. 3). First it meant cruelty, Ahaz 'even sacrificed his son in the fire'. This evil cult of child sacrifice to the demon god Molech shows that such religion is heartless and offends not only God's law but the natural instincts of decent human beings. Paul describes this aspect of fallen human nature as 'senseless, faithless, heartless, ruthless' (Rom. 1:31). Turning from God does not lead to warm affectionate humanity. Though the LORD had driven out the nations and their despicable practices, Ahaz leads a revival of these pagan atrocities.

David had charged Solomon to walk in the ways embodied in Moses' words (1 Kings 2:3). Ahaz had no respect for these words and indeed no sense of history. The covenant promises are being broken deliberately and trampled upon.

The high places have often been mentioned as a sign of the imperfect obedience of earlier kings of Judah. In those instances, it was probably a failure to deal with the problem, perhaps the kings taking the line of least resistance. But here the verbs are singular: *he* worshipped and offered incense. Ahaz deliberately indulged in pagan worship. The reference to 'every spreading tree' (v. 4) probably relates to fertility rites and Ahaz' participation in these. This was not passive acceptance but deliberate and relentless pursuit.

Ahaz is nothing if not religious and this will be developed later in the chapter; even in Isaiah 7:12 we get this sense of 'piety'. But this is religion without Torah and simply a front for self-indulgence. The Davidic line has never been in greater danger and the fate of the nation hangs in the balance. Moses had said that if God's people indulged in the detestable ways of the nations driven out of the promised land, then they in turn would be vomited out of the promised land themselves (Lev. 18:28). Is that point now being reached?

Dangerous alliance (16:5-9)
We now turn from religion to politics, although the two are closely intertwined. The incident here is sometimes called the 'Syro-Ephraimite war'. The account in verses 5-6 is brief but cannot hide the fact that Judah is in serious trouble. Azariah/Uzziah had restored Elath to Judah (2 Chron. 26:2). Elath on the Red Sea was at the centre of important land and sea routes and its loss to Syria was a severe blow, both politically and economically. Chronicles also tells us Ahaz was under attack from the Edomites and the Philistines (2 Chron. 28:17-18). The situation is dire and Ahaz reacts in what no doubt he and his spin doctors saw as a shrewd and sophisticated political and military move: he appeals for help to Tiglath-Pileser. In doing so he seemingly invites the fox into the hen house.

However, if we look at this in the unfolding story we see that Ahaz is putting himself outside the covenant promises. Already he has been contrasted to David and now that contrast becomes stark. Ahaz says to the Assyrian king, 'I am your servant and your vassal'; here the ESV translation of 'vassal' as 'son' is more accurate and also deliberately recalls Yahweh's words to David in 2 Samuel 7:14 that the Davidic king would be Yahweh's son. The king of Judah gives to the king of Assyria the homage that belongs to Yahweh in spite of the warnings of Isaiah (Isa. 7:10-17).

This lack of faith is accompanied by a 'gift' (v. 8) which is a euphemism for 'bribe'. A bribe of silver and gold, temple artefacts no less. After all, if Ahaz is repudiating his loyalty to Yahweh, what do a few trinkets from the temple of a God he does not believe in matter? It seems to work. Tiglath-Pileser captures Damascus, kills its king and deports its inhabitants (see Amos 1:5).

Disobedient religion (16:10-18)

As always, there is a price to pay. Ahaz is now completely subservient to Tiglath-Pileser and goes to Damascus to meet him, no doubt to express his allegiance in person. This whole section concentrates on Ahaz' religious activities, for where a faith in the living God is absent, religious activity often fills the vacuum. There are some difficulties of interpretation here, but these should not be allowed to obscure the basic thrust of the passage which is that Ahaz is inventing his own religion. We have already been told that he followed the kings of Israel and here he shows himself as true successor to Jeroboam, the son of Nebat, who back in 1 Kings 12 invented his own alternative religion.

Commentators discuss whether the altar (v. 10) was *Assyrian* or *Syrian*. If Assyrian, it would be a sign of homage to the Assyrian gods. That is probably unlikely because Judah is still technically independent, rather than an Assyrian province. It is more likely that this was a Syrian altar which Ahaz took a fancy to. After all, this was an altar at Damascus. This might be confirmed by 2 Chronicles 28:23 which tell us that Ahaz offered sacrifices to the gods of Damascus. Ahaz obviously spent long enough in Damascus for Uriah the priest to build an altar to the specifications he sent. It is surely no accident that when genuine faith is absent that a near obsession with detail takes its place. Many who sit loose to the faith once delivered to the saints develop elaborate rules about vestments and a concern with ritual and church furniture.

Our writer makes it plain that this is a personal initiative of Ahaz as 'the king' is repeated three times in verse 12. He takes the initiative in offering sacrifices. In a parade of piety, he offers the prescribed sacrifices on this new altar (see e.g. Num. 15:5-12). Isaiah attacks the bringing of 'meaningless offerings' (Isa. 1:13) and surely here we have a classic example of that. The bronze altar is moved, perhaps no great matter in itself but it is to be used 'for seeking guidance' (v. 15) which implies a kind of superstitious ritual which ignores the plain Word of God.

There has also been debate about the role of Uriah the priest who twice (vv. 11 and 16) is said to have followed Ahaz' instructions to the letter. Some argue he is a fundamentally decent and honest man because he is mentioned in Isaiah 8:2 as a reliable witness. But all the Isaiah passage states is that he is a well-known figure who would authenticate a document. When we ask for a signature on a legal paper we do not inquire about the signatory's spiritual life. It is difficult to avoid the impression that Uriah is a 'yes-man' concerned for his own position.

Ahaz' other activities in verses 17-18 are not altogether clear. Did he need further metal for more tribute to Assyria? 1 Kings 7:27-33 speaks of metal basins and a bronze base of the Sea; these Ahaz treated with a cavalier disdain. In any case, Ahaz is asset-stripping the temple, designed for the glory of God, for other purposes.

The account of his further religious innovations in verse 18 goes further than ritualistic practice and temple furnishings. The 'Sabbath canopy' and 'royal entrance' may have been symbols both of orthodox worship and royal status which were now removed 'in deference to the king of Assyria'. Even if such changes were not imposed by Tiglath-Pileser, it is plain that in Ahaz' Judah, it is not the Word of Yahweh but the word of the king of Assyria which calls the tune. Great care would be taken not to offend the new overlord in any way.

Dawning of a new hope? (16:19-20)

Ahaz' reign is over and events have reached a sorry state. He has brought the Davidic kingdom to humiliating insignificance and we wonder about the future of the line of David. There is a new altar, a new streamlined temple and a new master. Ahaz sowed the wind, and Judah is reaping the whirlwind. But although it is not yet evident, there is hope in the last words of the chapter, 'And Hezekiah his son succeeded him as king'. We will have to wait another long chapter before we see that there is indeed hope. For the moment, though, the realisation that another son of David is on the throne is ground for hope. Ahaz, despite his best efforts, could not bring the curtain down on God's covenant promises.

From text to message

Getting the message clear: the theme
Among all the religious and political upheavals of this chapter is the underlying theme of who do we trust. Pressures and problems are inevitable and we need to be sure of who deserves our faith and loyalty.

Getting the message clear: the aim
The aim is to encourage faith especially when we are faced with gigantic problems which fill our horizon. It is said of Moses in Hebrews 11:27 that 'he persevered because he saw him who is invisible'. The seen problems will always threaten to loom larger than the unseen God and only the perspective of faith will restore the balance.

A way in
A nineteenth-century pioneer missionary to the New Hebrides, John Paton, spent a lot of time translating parts of the Bible into the native languages. One day he was struggling to find a word which would express the true meaning of faith. At that moment one of his associates came in from working in the fields and sat down thankfully saying he was glad to find something to rest his weight on. Paton immediately thought that was the expression he was looking for. Faith is someone or something on whom we can rest our weight.

Here Ahaz rests his weight on politics, religion and diplomatic alliances. Of course there are all kinds of secondary things in which we have faith, society could not function without a degree of mutual trust in people's promises, the value of money, the transport system, law and order and the like. But none of these things are infallible and our lives need something to rest on when these fail.

Ideas for application

+ When we reject the Word of God and fail to learn from history we are heading for disaster. We too easily forget that God judges His own people when they disobey.

+ False religion may appear to be liberal but is in fact heartless. Everything is swept under the carpet and never dealt with.

+ When we trust in worldly alliances rather than the Lord we end up in greater danger. This is true in the personal and social world as well as the political. We are all tempted by the outward and visible.

+ We easily become tempted to doctor our worship to make it more exciting.[2] I'm not talking about different orders of service, local customs or adaptations to make what we do accessible to everyone. Rather about the temptation to water down the message, become totally horizontal and see the aim of worship as meeting each other rather than the Lord and seeing relevance as having a controlling veto rather than having its proper pragmatic importance.

+ Hope even despite human failings. Despite Ahaz's best efforts he cannot destroy God's covenant promises.

---

2.   Davis, *2 Kings Ch 21*, pp. 227-36.

We need to keep in mind the overall story. While we must avoid tedious repetition and saying of every king, 'he's not the one' yet we must remember that everything is driven by the promise to David. Thus with Ahaz we see another attempt of Satan to destroy the line of David and prevent the coming of the Messiah.

Suggestions for preaching

We might want to follow the outline above under the four headings suggested. If we do that, then the fourth point would be a brief footnote pointing to but not attempting to cover in depth the material in chapters 18 and 19.

We could follow Ralph Davis' outline which divides the chapter into four similar sections but with different headings and slightly different emphases. Both these follow the flow of the narrative and place it in context.

Suggestions for teaching

Questions to help understand the passage

1. Why is Ahaz contrasted with David? (v. 2)

2. What do we expect from Ahaz since he follows in the footsteps of the kings of Israel?

3. Why is Ahaz afraid of Syria and Israel?

4. Why does it seem a good move at first for Ahaz to call for the king of Assyria's help?

5. What does verse 10ff show about Ahaz' attitude to the temple?

6. Is it fair to see Uriah the priest as a 'yes-man'? (vs. 11 and 16)

7. What does verse 18b suggest about Ahaz' priorities?

8. What is the significance of the mention of Hezekiah's succession? (v. 20)

Questions to help apply the passage

1. What do verses 2 and 3 suggest will happen when the Word of God is rejected?

2. What does verse 7 suggest about Ahaz' faith? How can we avoid falling into this trap?

3. Why does the altar matter? You might like to look at Hebrews 13:10 and reflect on the significance of atonement.

4. What happens to our faith when we depart from the Word of God?

5. How does the end of the chapter show that God keeps His covenant promises?

14

What Happens When Grace is Rejected (17)

Introduction

The end for the northern kingdom has come at last. We last saw Israel in chapter 15, lurching from one crisis to another, but this has now passed the point of no return. The atmosphere is bleak and the events unfold with a stark inevitability. A number of issues are emphasised, the first is the ruthlessness of power politics with Israel's final weak leader brushed aside by the powerful king of Assyria. The unadorned phrases which recount the fall of Samaria and the deportation of the people have a stern note like the pealing of funeral bells.

That power is embodied in the king of Assyria, who is mentioned six times in verses 3 to 6, and Assyria is to dominate the story. Indeed, this is to be the international background for the next few chapters and at this moment it appears that it is curtains not just for the North but also for the South.

Listening to the text

Context and Structure

It is important that we do not see these events as driven by the power of Assyria. Verse 7 gives us our bearings, 'All this took place because the Israelites sinned against the LORD their God'. The events of this chapter flow directly from the prophetic words back in 1 Kings 14:10-16 spoken to Jeroboam the first king of Israel. Not only is the doom of Jeroboam's own dynasty foretold but the ultimate fate of the nation to be 'scattered beyond the River.'[1] More than two hundred years had passed since Ahijah the prophet had said this but it is now being fulfilled, another example of how the prophetic Word is not limited by time.

The chapter has four main divisions:

* Reaping what is sown (17:1-6)

* Why this disaster happened (17:7-17)

* Neglected warnings (17:18-23)

* What is true worship? (17:24-41)

Working through the text

Reaping what is sown (17:1-6)

Hosea, one of the prophets who had warned the northern kingdom, had warned that sowing the wind would reap the whirlwind (Hosea 8:7) and this whirlwind is now howling. Two elements stand out in this brief chronicle. The first is the continuing weakness of Israel's leaders. Hoshea, the last king of Israel, is seen in less than flattering terms. We are told he was not as bad as his predecessors but plainly

---

1.   Usually 'River' with a capital letter refers to the Euphrates.

did nothing to remedy their failures. Hoshea was also politically inept and foolishly tried to form an alliance with the Pharaoh which led to his own imprisonment and the end of his kingdom. A further irony is that Hoshea is another form of Joshua and means 'Saviour'. This hapless man was no saviour but the last of a doomed and discredited line.

The second element, already noted, is the terrifying power of Assyria who invaded, conquered and deported. Yet, as we shall see in 19:25-8, behind the Assyrian invasion is a greater power, Yahweh, king of the nations. God is using Assyria to punish His people but they too will experience His judgement (this is developed more fully in Isaiah 10:5-34). That is for the future and at the moment the picture is as bleak as it could be.

Why this disaster happened (17:7-17)

The explanation for this catastrophe is much fuller than the brief note of the event itself. This is deliberate because it would be all too easy to interpret what happened as simply a weak and badly governed petty kingdom succumbing to a ruthless military machine led by single-minded warlords. On the human level that is what happened but that is not the ultimate reason for the fall of Samaria. The defeat of Israel stemmed from their rejection of a gracious God who had rescued them centuries before from Pharaoh of Egypt; another reason why Hoshea's attempted alliance with Egypt was so pathetic. These verses are no random listing of sins and failures but they go to the very heart of Israel's rejection of the Covenant Lord.

At the heart of Israel's apostasy was a rejection of grace. The rescue from slavery at the Exodus, the supreme example of God's gracious covenant with them, no longer moved them to gratitude and praise. Indeed, amazing grace was greeted with overweening arrogance. This is a warning to us. When people begin to drift away from the Lord it is usually a result of turning our backs on grace. Without grace we are on our own and thus turn to godlets to fill the vacuum.

This leads to wholesale idolatry and we can read examples of this tale in places like the book of Judges. The nature of idolatry is spelled out in verses 8-12. Idolatry is never a neutral thing but results in a particular lifestyle following Canaanite and other practices, some copied from the nations expelled from the land and others introduced by their own kings, not least by Ahab. The word 'secretly' (v. 9) is particularly interesting because the practices mentioned are in the public eye. Probably this not only refers to secret activities but to what the people believed in the secrecy of their own hearts which were no longer loyal to Yahweh.

The notorious high places, a perpetual snare to the kings of both Israel and Judah, dotted the landscape both in city and country and the Baalistic sacred stones and Asherah poles were everywhere. The less worship has to do with the heart the more it relies on outward symbols. Moses had said 'you are a people holy to Yahweh your God' (Deut. 7:6) but the nation's history instead revealed a frantic desire to be as like the other nations as possible.

None of this happened without continual warnings and appeals from Yahweh through His prophets. Not only did they reject the Torah of Moses, they rejected the prophets sent by God. Here (v. 13) Judah is mentioned, a point to which we will return. The earlier parts of this book have highlighted the great prophetic ministries of Elijah and Elisha, and more recently we know that Amos and Hosea had spoken powerfully into the situation. A host of named and unnamed prophets had faithfully given witness to Yahweh but the rush to ruin had continued. They were without excuse.

The progression of their disobedience is outlined in verses 14-17. There is first a failure to listen (v. 14) which is a product of stubborn self-will. Then there is deliberate rejection (v. 15) both of Moses and the prophets. This, in turn, leads to going after false gods, which then infects the people with falsehood and plunges them into futility and worthlessness. Idolatry always opens the door to unreality. Without the clear Word of God to guide them they resort to imitating the nations. They also no doubt prided themselves on being progressive but in fact they reverted to the old idolatry of golden calves and discredited Baal-worship. They descended to the darkest sides of paganism, sacrificing children and giving themselves to the enthusiastic pursuit of evil. The expression 'sold themselves' (v. 17) has already been used of Ahab (1 Kings 21:20, 25). The author of Hebrews warns us that this is no mere ancient history, 'If they did not escape when they refused him who warned them on earth, how much less will we, if we turn away from him who warns us from heaven?' (Heb. 12:25)

Neglected warnings (17:18-23)
Notice the judgment of the Lord: 'removed', 'rejected', 'gave them into the hands of plunderers', 'thrust them from his presence' (vv. 18-20). But what is particularly interesting is the mention of Judah. When Judah's exile comes in chapter 25 there is virtually no theological comment, only a laconic statement, 'So Judah went into captivity, away from her own land' (25:21b). So here this passage is doing double

duty in providing theological comment on the exiles of the
two nations. This is in keeping with the overall picture of
the slide to exile. Judgment began when north and south
were divided back in Rehoboam's time (1 Kings 12) and
will not be completed until both nations are exiled and
then beyond exile reunited and returned (see Ezek. 37).
The same disobedience which destroyed Israel is to destroy
Judah, indeed Judah is to be worse (see the powerful allegory
in Ezekiel 23 where Oholibah (Jerusalem) is worse than
Oholah (Samaria)). Both are removed from their homeland
in an exile which is spiritual as well as geographical.

What is true worship? (17:24-41).
Here we have a picture of what religion without Torah
means. The king of Assyria does not leave the land empty
but repopulates it with people from other conquered
provinces. This process probably took some considerable
time and populated the former Israel with pagans. Some
native Israelites would have remained but they had been so
long accustomed to paganism that we must suppose they
would notice little difference. The incursion of lions was
seen as divine retribution for failure to 'worship the god of
that country' and a priest was sent back from Assyria to
'teach what the god of the country requires' (v. 27). Provan
is probably right when he says that this passage is full of
irony[2] and represents how the people of the time saw the
situation rather than what the author believes. The priest,
as part of the old Samaria establishment, is hardly likely
to be teaching the words of Moses. He sets up shop in
Bethel where Jeroboam I had established his syncretistic
worship (1 Kings 12:31-3). What he teaches is not about

---

2.   Provan pp. 250-1.

Yahweh who made heaven and earth but about 'the god of the country'.

Meanwhile human religion carried along on its merry way (vv. 29-33). This was human invention; notice the repetition of the word 'made'. Whatever the returned priest had taught no one believed in revelation and indeed, again following Jeroboam, they appointed their own priests to pander to their whims. Lip service was paid to Yahweh (v. 33) but for purposes of living and behaving everyone did what was right in their own eyes. 'Worship' had become self-indulgence and a total ignoring of revelation.

The author inserts into all of this a reminder of what true covenant worship is. The Lord must speak to us before we speak to Him; indeed, we would have nothing at all to say to God unless He first spoke to us. There is a reminder of God's gracious and exclusive covenant and the great historical events of the Exodus and of the giving of the Decalogue. Yet, even with deportation to Assyria now a reality there is still persistent unbelief expressed in lip service to Yahweh and the lifestyle of paganism. This hardens into persistent unbelief as generation follows generation (vv. 40, 41). Yet the covenant realities, underlined again in verses 34-9, will not go away and remain as a challenge to those who will humble themselves and seek the face of the Lord they have rejected.

From text to message

Getting the message clear: the theme
The overriding theme is the rejection of grace. It is not fundamentally about this or that law but about disloyalty

to the relationship with the Covenant Lord from where all other sins and failures flow.

Getting the message clear: the aim

The absolute priority of a relationship with the Lord. Without this worship we will degenerate into pious phrases and living will be about what suits us rather than obeying what God has revealed.

A way in

In C.S. Lewis' *The Voyage of the Dawn Treader* the unpleasant, but ultimately reformed Eustace Clarence Scrubbs pontificates that 'a star is a huge ball of flaming gas', to which the wise old man Ramandu replies, 'Even in your world, my son, that is not what a star is but only what it is made of'.[3] This is a helpful distinction when we approach a chapter like this which is made of power politics, militarism, apostasy and pride. But what it shows us is grace being rejected but not ultimately defeated. Thus it has great relevance to us. A true appreciation of grace will save us from sin and bring us to glory.

Ideas for application

+ This is one of many passages throughout the book which reminds us that the Word of God will be fulfilled even after a long time; in this case over two hundred years. Many faithful servants of God have laboured for many years in difficult and dark places and seen little for their efforts but so often that has been the essential sowing for reaping to be possible in later generations.

---

3. C.S. Lewis, *The Voyage of the Dawn Treader*, (Folio Society. 2012), p. 194.

We need to remember as well that the preaching of judgment will have results.

+ Again weak leadership is exposed as central to the overall failure of God's people. The qualified negative that Hoshea was not as bad as some of his predecessors is itself a sign that the kingdom is doomed.

+ God judges His own people when they rebel. Moses promised not only blessings for faithfulness to the covenant but curses for disobedience (Deut. 28:15-68.)

+ Rejection of grace leads to pride and a contempt for the Lord who saved us. This in turn makes it easy to disobey His commands. Idolatry, in all its varied forms, happens when we leave our first love. This leads to a lukewarm state where everything is subject to what we want. The church at Laodicea is a stark warning of that danger (Rev. 3:14-22.)

+ God's Word is persistent but there comes a time when continual rejection means that the point of no return is passed. The prophet Amos, speaking into the situation of this chapter, is told by the Lord to stop pleading for the salvation of Israel: 'I am setting a plumb-line among my people Israel; I will spare them no longer' (Amos 7:9.)

+ It is possible to pay lip service to the Lord without truly worshipping Him and to live a totally godless lifestyle.

+ God's grace cannot ultimately fail (v. 30) but His people need to come to Him in repentance and faith.

Suggestions for preaching

This is not the easiest chapter to preach on but it is essential not to ignore it not least because of its application to Judah's exile at the end of the book.

Sermon 1

We could take the four suggested sections as an outline and preach on the chapter as a whole carefully summarising the major themes and using the title *What happens when grace is rejected.*

Reaping what is sown (vv. 1-6)
Bad leadership and God raising Assyria in judgment.

Turning away from the Lord (vv. 7-17)
Despising the covenant.

Ignoring the warnings (vv. 18-23)
God's messengers rejected.

Empty worship (vv. 24-41)
Imitating the world and persisting in unbelief.

Sermons 2 and 3

We could preach two sermons: one on verses 1-17 and one on verses 18-41 using the above outline and developing it more fully.

Suggestions for teaching

Questions to help understand the passage

1. Why is the fall of Israel described so briefly (vv. 1-6)? Relate this to the long descriptions of idolatry earlier in the book.

2. How does the author emphasise the danger of the king of Assyria?

3. Why is the Exodus mentioned (v. 7 and again in vv. 34-9)?

4. Why does the author mention Judah at this point (v. 18-20)?

5. What was the significance of Jeroboam (vv. 21-2)?

6. Who were the prophets of verse 23?

7. How do we know that the priest sent back from Assyria was unlikely to give proper teaching (vv. 27-8)?

8. What is the significance of mentioning the Decalogue here (vv. 37-38)?

9. Is there a hint of hope in verse 39?

Questions to help apply the passage

1. Why is it foolish to try to fight Assyria with Assyrian methods? Think about what Assyria might mean in our situations.

2. In what ways are we in danger of treating salvation lightly as the people here despised the Exodus?

3. We do not set up images and 'high places', but are always in danger of idolatry (1 John 5:21). Think of some of the idols to which Evangelicals are prone.

4. Verse 29ff are a picture of what happens when the Word of God is not properly taught. What happens and how can we guard against the same dangers?

PART THREE:
THE CLOSING YEARS OF JUDAH
(2 KINGS 18-25)

15

DAVID COMES AGAIN (18)

Introduction

Right on the brink of the abyss experienced by Israel in the previous chapter, it appears that Judah is sure to suffer the same fate, until the glimmers of hope in 16:20 explode into flooding rays of light-filled hope. The excitement and surprise of this chapter recall Psalm 126, whose primary reference is to the LORD restoring the fortunes of Zion after the Exile but that relief is foreshadowed here as He rescues Zion first from idolatry and unbelief and then from the Assyrian menace. After downright bad kings, notably Ahaz (chapter 16) and mediocre 'yes but' kings such as Joash and Amaziah (chapters 12-13) a young man of twenty-five comes to the throne who recalls the great days of David. We need to go back to Asa (1 Kings 15:11) to find a king who 'did what was right in the eyes of the LORD as his father David had done'; and that was two hundred years before.

But here is something different. 'There was no one like him among all the kings of Judah, either before or after him' (v. 5). The secret was that he trusted Yahweh and, unlike his father, Ahaz was a man of faith. Everything he was and did flowed from this. We need to realise that a man like this is a genuine foreshadowing of the King who was to come. Hezekiah was not the Messiah but his reign gave a genuine, if limited, glimpse of the kingdom.

We come here to the fifth section of the book (18:1-23, 30) which I entitled 'Reformers and Wreckers' (see Introduction p. 31). The history now is of the kingdom of Judah with the two best kings, but also the worst. Good leaders can delay judgment but not finally avert it and sandwiched between the two worthiest sons of David to sit on his throne there is the worst whose behaviour makes the Exile inevitable.

Listening to the text

Context and Structure

Chapter 17 had spoken of the forthcoming exile of Judah (17:18-20) and we would have expected that event to follow almost immediately, but in one of the Lord's most surprising interventions what happens instead is a time of sweeping reform. This is all the more surprising considering that Hezekiah was son of Ahaz and indeed probably co-regent with him before becoming sole king.[1] Where did his desire for godliness come from? It seems certain that Isaiah's influence was crucial and the denunciation of false religion in Isaiah 1 speaks of precisely the abuses Hezekiah dealt with. There was also the influence of Micah, mentioned in

---

1.   See Wiseman p.272.

Jeremiah 26:18-19. Hezekiah is specifically contrasted with Ahaz who did not follow in the ways of David (16:2). Here we have an outline of what the new Davidic king looks like.

The chapter develops in four movements:

+ The new David (18:1-8)

+ The bleak alternative (18:9-12)

+ Falling at the first hurdle? (18:13-16)

+ Goliath threatens David (18:17-37)

Working through the text

The new David (18:1-8)
Here is what happens when a true Davidic king reigns. The mainspring of his actions was faith in Yahweh and this was no mere private opinion but resulted in vigorous reform and a thorough cleansing of the nation's life. Three aspects of this welcome change are outlined. The first is the thorough reformation of Judah's worship. At long last here is a king who removed the high places which had proved a stumbling block for so long.[2] Other aspects of paganism such as the sacred stones and Asherah poles suffered the same fate. But his reform was not confined to paganism only but also to the destruction of the bronze snake which Moses had used in Numbers 21:4-9. This artefact had once pointed the way to the true God but now had become a snare as if it had power within itself. We have already noticed that Isaiah not only condemns idolatry but the perversion of God-given rituals (see esp. Isa. 1:10-17), so here Hezekiah recognises the danger of objects being more valued than the reality to which they point. False religion always focusses

---

2.   The text is emphatic 'It was he' or 'He was the one'.

on material objects and thus any reformation needs to get beyond these.

The second aspect of Hezekiah's reformation was a renewed and sincere obedience to the Word of God. This flowed from his faith in Yahweh and was no mere verbal commitment. He 'held fast' to Yahweh (v. 6); this Word is used of a man and his wife (Gen. 2:24) and thus suggests full commitment to the covenant. The Word is also sadly used of Solomon holding fast to his many wives (1 Kings 11:2). Hezekiah here is following David's charge to Solomon (1 Kings 2:3-4) which set the theme for the book and shows Hezekiah's determination to turn the people back to the Word of God.[3] This is a classic example of how faithfulness to God involves, indeed springs from, faithfulness to His Word.

The third echo of David was Hezekiah's military success, unparalleled since the time of the great king himself. The key to this was that 'the LORD was with him' (v. 7), echoing what was said of David (e.g. 1 Sam. 16:18). Thus he rejected the Assyrian influence which his father Ahaz had so readily accepted (16:7-14). Also the defeat of the Philistines recalls the victories of David.

So there is no need to despair in times of darkness because God is always at work, even after godless Ahaz we now have a true Davidic king who is to turn the nation back to God. The Lord is continually confounding our pessimism with His total relevance to every situation including the darkest.

---

3.   This also shows that the classic liberal idea that the Pentateuch, especially Deuteronomy, was the product of a reforming party in Josiah's time will not hold water. Almost certainly the words of Moses had been suppressed by Ahaz as they were again to be by Manasseh.

The bleak alternative (18:9-12)

There is another account of the fall of the northern kingdom which has been described already in 17:1-6, this is probably here to remind us of how Hezekiah was operating in a most discouraging situation. It is possible that when the Assyrians captured Samaria they may have sent a division southward to shake their armed fist at Jerusalem.[4] In any case, this brought the Assyrians uncomfortably near Jerusalem and would no doubt cause real alarm.

Verse 12 reminds us of the reason for the fall of the northern kingdom: it was the violation of the covenant which Hezekiah is busily restoring in the south. We would therefore expect a different fate for Judah, or we would at least if we had not read 17:19-20 which, despite this upturn, still hangs over Judah's future. The story is about to take a different turn and that will occupy our attention until the end of chapter 19.

Falling at the first hurdle? (18:13-16)

This new David is going to have to face Goliath who makes his appearance in the fourteenth year of Hezekiah's reign which was the year 701 B.C. The new century opens with storms brewing for Judah. Sennacherib was making his way down the coast from Phoenicia through the Philistine territory from which he would launch his attack on Judah.[5] But surely a righteous king will be spared the assaults

---

4.   This may be the thrust of the poetic description of the advance of the Assyrians on Zion (Isa. 10:28-32) which speaks of the Assyrians advancing from the north whereas Sennacherib approached Jerusalem from the south-west.

5.   See Wiseman pp. 273-4 for background.

which brought down the northern kingdom. This does not happen and the story unfolds very differently.

But what about verses 14-18? Does this man of faith fall at the first hurdle and like his father Ahaz succumb to the bully? Notice first the different language used by the two men. Ahaz had said to the Assyrian king that he was his 'servant and son' (16:7), thus deliberately rejecting the covenant with Yahweh in favour of one with Assyria. Hezekiah makes no such concession (v. 14) but rather attempts to buy time. Regrettably he sends the temple treasures to Sennacherib, which he had done so much to restore (see 2 Chron. 29). So this is a serious lapse in faith. But that is what it is, a lapse, and we must see it in the light of 18:1-8 which covers Hezekiah's reign, including the further lapse in chapter 20. Like David, he is flawed but faithful. Even the strongest faith has its times of doubt and crisis and we must not imagine that we are stronger than we are.

Goliath threatens David (18:17-37)

In any case Hezekiah's attempt to placate the Assyrians does not work because Sennacherib is a cheat as well as a bully and wants to destroy Jerusalem as he had the other cities of Judah. The story continues to the end of chapter 19 but is too long to be conveniently treated in one chapter. I will suggest at the end of the treatment of the next chapter on chapter 19 a possible outline for preaching the narrative as a whole. It is fascinating to compare this story with 1 Samuel 17, the famous story of David and Goliath. In both stories, the emphasis is on words, boasting words and words of faith. In both the conclusion is brief and decisive and in both the nature of God and the gods is at stake.

It is from the area of the valley of Elah that the Assyrian Goliath advances on David's city. They stopped at 'the aqueduct of the upper pool' (v. 17) where some thirty years before Isaiah had met Ahaz and challenged him to have faith in Yahweh (Isaiah 7:3ff.) This is to be the scene of a much greater challenge to faith.

Sennacherib sends three of his top brass: the Tartan or Commander in Chief; the Rabsaris, probably the chief royal adviser and the Rabshakeh, probably a senior official close to the king. This delegation is clearly intended to impress and intimidate. They are arrogant; 'they called for the king' (v. 18) but here Hezekiah shows his true mettle; he will not deal with underlings. If Sennacherib will not negotiate personally, nor will Hezekiah and thus high officials of his court go out to meet the Assyrians. The subsequent passage is a speech by the Rabshakeh (vv. 19-25); a reply by Eliakim (v. 26) and a further speech by the Rabshakeh (vv. 27-36). Words are the issue here and we need to notice a number of things.

First we remember this is one of the unifying themes of the book: the words of God and the words of humans and how they relate. The Rabshakeh is no mere swaggering bully; he is a spin doctor who knows how to use words to persuade and manipulate. He exposes the weakness of the Judaeans and makes many shrewd observations. He exposes the unreliability of Egypt and the weakness of that once great power. Isaiah also denounces those who look to Egypt for help (Isa. 31). There would no doubt be a pro-Egyptian party in Judah but there is no evidence that

Hezekiah associated with it[6] (v. 21). The Rabshakeh shows essentially pagan thinking when he attributes Hezekiah's reforms to be taking action against the local god and thus foolish of Hezekiah to expect any help from that god (v. 22). The Rabshakeh sneers at the obvious weakness of Judah, who had so few men that they could not even provide riders if they were given horses (v. 24). And with brazen affrontery he claims that he was attacking Jerusalem at the command of Yahweh (v. 25).

Four times (vv. 19, 28, 30, 31) Rabshakeh calls Sennacherib the 'king of Assyria', two of these add the Word 'great'. Yet he never calls Hezekiah 'king' and tries to devalue him by calling him simply 'Hezekiah'. He scorns Hezekiah's standing and tries to belittle him in front of the people. The Rabshakeh then glosses over the miseries of deportation (vv. 31-2) and speaks as if Assyria was a mirror image of Judah, a place of prosperity and bounty. This contravenes God's Word where the land promised to the patriarchs was such that there was no land like their own which pointed to the 'better country' (Heb. 11:16).

So far the Rabshakeh has sounded rather convincing, so much so that Eliakim asks him to speak in Aramaic which the people on the wall did not understand (v. 27). The plausible mask slips as the Assyrian warns of the horrors of a siege but then quickly goes on to speak of the attractiveness of life in Assyria. But then he makes his fatal mistake (vv. 32b-35) as he compares Yahweh to the gods of other nations destroyed by Sennacherib. The identity of these places in verse 34 is not certain but they

---

6.   Isaiah 31 cannot be dated precisely but is thought to belong to Hezekiah's reign and may indeed belong to his early years before his reforms began to take effect.

were probably in Syria and for good measure he mentions the capture of Samaria. The Assyrian gods had triumphed over these lesser gods and Yahweh would meet the same fate. We shall see how that boast fared in chapter 19.

However, all unknown to himself the Rabshakeh had focussed on the twin themes which run through the story and indeed the Bible. The first is the theme of trust (vv. 19, 20, 22, 24, 30). He, of course, had not had the advantage of reading verses 1-8. He describes Hezekiah's confidence as 'mere words' (v. 20) but in chapter 19 we are to hear the words of the living God Himself. The second is 'save' or 'deliver' (vv. 32-35). This is the great Word of the Exodus and now again we are to see whether God can deliver His people.

Yet the ending of the chapter is downbeat and instead of words there is silence and the Judaean officials tear their clothes, the traditional sign of mourning. They do not know yet how the events of chapter 19 will unfold. There never has been a greater need for faith. Sennacherib is coming nearer and nearer.

From text to message

Getting the message clear: the theme
A second David has come to the fight and brought new hope and vision but he is in danger both from his own weakness and a terrifying enemy. Like chapter 16 the important theme of who do we trust is explored.

Getting the message clear: the aim
The aim of this chapter is probably best expressed in the words used of Moses in Hebrews 11:27, 'he persevered because he saw him who is invisible'. A gigantic enemy is all

too visible and can only be met by faith in a God who has promised to protect His people.

A way in

We need to try to convey something of the exciting and revolutionary nature of the passage. Other similar times could be referred to: e.g. the Wesleys and Whitefield or the coming to life of a moribund church driven by the Word of God. We would also need to emphasise that such times never come without opposition both internal and external.

Ideas for application

* We rightly reject the idea that we can bring about revival by our own efforts but it is all too easy to swing to the opposite extreme and develop a kind of unbelieving pessimism which imagines that God is unable to do great things. We do not know when God will choose to revive His work nor must we limit the power of the Spirit.

* All true reformation comes from a commitment to the Lord and His Word. We must continually cultivate this relationship with the Lord as His Spirit takes His Word and sets our hearts on fire.

* Here as always in our applications we need to look for the idols in our own hearts and churches rather than simply denouncing those of others.

* Faith is not a crutch as some have cynically argued but an opening of our hearts in their weakness to a powerful God. We depend on Him, not on our faith which often wobbles as Hezekiah's does here.

- Faith and godliness do not make us immune to attack as the book of Job demonstrates. Here the man of faith is subjected to the same pressures and attacks as those who have turned their back on God.

- Faith is realistic; it does not boast and swagger but instead recognises how weak we all are.

Suggestions for preaching

This chapter, along with chapter 19, is one of the richest parts of the book and there are different ways in which we might approach preaching it.

Sermon 1

This would take the chapter as a whole under some such heading as 'New Hope and New Danger'

Three scenes:

- A new David and a radical reformation (vv. 1-8).

- New dangers and a panicky response (vv. 9-16).

- A dangerous threat to king and people (vv. 17-37).

Sermon 2

This would take the first eight verses as a separate sermon:

David comes again (18:1-8)

Introduction emphasising that here is someone radically different – emphasis on trust and covenant faithfulness.

- Restores true worship – inward reality and not outward show.

- Restores Word of God to its true place.

- Rebels against king of Assyria and defeats the ancient enemy, the Philistines.

Gathering Darkness (18:9-37)
Hezekiah's situation was not ideal.

+ Threats from Assyria who come within a few miles of Jerusalem.

+ Reminder of why northern kingdom fell.

+ Wobble of faith.

+ The enemy almost at the gates.

My own feeling is that 18:1-8 probably should be preached on their own because the description of Hezekiah is so important in itself and it is a great reminder of the key themes of the book. 18:17-19:37 is a continuous narrative and could perhaps be preached together. See comments in next chapter for suggestions of how to do that.

Suggestions for teaching

Questions to help understand the passage

1. Why is the introduction to Hezekiah's reign (18:1-8) longer than that of many other kings?

2. What is the significance of the phrase 'just as his father David had done'? (v. 3)

3. Why are the Philistines (v. 8) particularly mentioned?

4. What is the point of verse 12?

5. What is the significance of the mention of the temple treasures?

6. Why is 'the king of Assyria' mentioned so many times?

7. How do you think the Rabshakeh knows so much, along with misinformation, of what is happening in Judah? (vv. 19-25)

8. What is the point of mentioning the other national gods? (vv. 33-5)

9. Why does Hezekiah command the people to be silent? (v. 36)

10. How do the Jewish officials show the seriousness of the situation?

Questions to help apply the passage

1. What do verses 5 and 6 tell us about the life of faith? What is its relationship to obedience?

2. Compare verses 7 and 13. What is the relationship between faithfulness and success and why is this surprising in the light of verse 12?

3. Why do Hezekiah's actions in verses 14-16 not disqualify him from being a man of faith?

4. Why does the author tell us that the Assyrian delegation stopped at 'the aqueduct of the upper pool'? (v. 17) Read Isaiah 7:3ff and reflect on how this bears on the life of faith.

5. Comment on the use of the words 'trust' and 'deliver' in the Rabshakeh's speeches. Is he, like Caiaphas (John 11:49-52), speaking more wisely than he knows?

6. How do verses 33-5 expose the sham of pagan religion?

16

THE GOD OF JACOB IS OUR FORTRESS (19)

Introduction

Some readers will have visited the Assyrian rooms in the British Museum. In one of these rooms is a splendid series of wall reliefs depicting Sennacherib's siege and capture of a city. An inscription reads, 'Sennacherib, King of Assyria, sitting on his throne while the spoil of the city of Lachish passed before him'. These came from Sennacherib's principal palace in Nineveh, raising the question as to why it was thought necessary to record in detail the capture of a remote mountain town which no-one in Assyria would probably have heard of up to that time. The Assyrian spin doctors knew what they were doing: This was propaganda to conceal the fact that the Assyrians had failed in their main objective which was to take Jerusalem.

Yet Jerusalem was in a perilous situation. Lachish, Judah's second city, was reduced to rubble and an attempted attack on the Assyrians by Egypt failed. This was probably associated with Sennacherib's attack on Libnah (v. 8) which probably was between Lachish and Gath. The Cushite king who became the Pharaoh threatened the Assyrians but was not strong enough for a major engagement and returned home. Meanwhile the Assyrian army was drawing nearer and nearer to Jerusalem which looked doomed and which drew more boasting from Sennacherib in a letter sent to Hezekiah which repeated the threats of the Rabshakeh.

This is one of the most powerful narratives in the book and in many respects recalls Elijah's stand against the prophets of Baal back in 1 Kings 18. Here is the same contest about who is the true God. The same believing prayer as opposed to trusting false gods and a powerful prophetic voice. Here again faith is tested to the limit. Another story, this time of Elisha in Dothan (2 Kings 6) and the power of the angels of God has interesting parallels.

Listening to the Text

Context and Structure

The story began in the previous chapter and has strong narrative flow. There are all the marks of a good story: suspense, unexpected twists and vivid characterisation. It is also a story of human weakness and God's power, this episode so easily could have marked the end and exile of Judah. But it is also a story of faith. Unlike his father Ahaz (2 Kings 16:7-11), Hezekiah trusts in Yahweh rather than capitulating and thus stands firm in faith (cf. Isa. 7:10).

Attention has already been drawn to the parallels with 1 Samuel 17 and especially in the arrogant boasting and taunting of Goliath. Here, in fact from 18:19 the mocking rhetoric of the Rabshakeh and his master is at the heart of the story. This is matched by the prayerful words of

Hezekiah and the powerful words of Isaiah. The story is at the very heart of the book's major concern with the power of God's words and the often ineffective words of humans.

The narrative unfolds in four sections:

+ Hezekiah's appeal for help (19:1-13)

+ Hezekiah's prayer of faith (19:14-19)

+ Isaiah's powerful words (19:20-34)

+ The judgment on Assyria and its king (19:35-37)

Working through the text

Hezekiah's appeal for help (19:1-13)

The story flows seamlessly from the end of chapter 18; as the boastful words of the Rabshakeh are relayed to Hezekiah, he tears his clothes, like three characters at the end of chapter 18. 'King' Hezekiah is given here the title the Assyrian denied him. Tearing clothes and wearing sackcloth was a sign of mourning and repentance (e.g. Dan. 9:3; Neh. 9:1). Hezekiah had got rid of the idolatrous symbols and emphasised a heart engagement with God but these outward symbols are mere window dressing and what he now does and says shows how genuine this reformation was. He sends messengers not to his military commanders but to the prophet Isaiah, an action that many of his predecessors fail to take.

Hezekiah's words are full of grief; grief for the children who will perish or not be born if Assyria destroys Jerusalem. But more fundamentally the Assyrians have 'ridiculed the Living God' (the mockery theme again). Hezekiah also says that Yahweh may intervene; not meaning that he doubts God's power but that he will not presume. Similarly, when he says to Isaiah 'your' God, this does not mean he has no personal faith but that he recognises the prophet as the channel of true revelation.

Isaiah's reply is punchy and firm.[1] Again there is the emphasis on the blasphemous words of the Assyrians. Also, in a wonderful putdown, the macho men of Assyria are described as 'underlings' (v. 6). Perhaps the report is of Egyptian manoeuvres and at this stage Isaiah is not predicting precisely what will happen but does anticipate his later words on Yahweh's control of history (vv. 25-6).

Indeed the situation still looks bleak and is becoming bleaker, which is the point of verses 8-13. Egypt had failed to turn the Assyrians back and Hezekiah is treated to a gloating repetition of the superiority of the Assyrian war machine and the failure of the gods of the nations to protect their cities. Hezekiah is deluded if he thinks that his god is any different and his city will disappear into the same dustbin as the others. The Assyrian approach continues and does seem to mock Isaiah's confidence and Hezekiah's faith.

Hezekiah's prayer of faith (19:14-19)

Hezekiah could have prayed anywhere but the significance of taking Sennacherib's letter to the temple of the LORD should not be ignored. This is the particular place where Yahweh, whom the highest heavens cannot contain (1 Kings 8:27), particularly places His name and from His dwelling in heaven hears when His servants pray on earth (1 Kings 8:30). Also, there is the deliberate contrast between the temple of Sennacherib's god (v. 37).

---

1.   In Ralph Davis' delightful phrase, 'Isaiah is not into 'perhapses''. Davis p. 276.

This prayer, although short, is one of the great prayers of the Bible. It gives us many insights into the nature of God and the nature of prayer. It is not that 'prayer changes things', a pious sounding but misleading phrase which implies that our prayers are more important than the One to whom we pray. Rather prayer puts us in touch with the God who changes things and this is the God to whom Hezekiah prays. Prayer is a recognition of human helplessness calling on God's help. The visible problem is brought to the invisible God. So who is this God to whom Hezekiah prays?

He is Yahweh the covenant God, committed to His people by promises which He will not break. He is on the throne; a fact unknown to Sennacherib as he sat on his throne among the ruins of Lachish. The cherubim on the ark of the covenant showed His presence among His people and the hosts of heaven around Him. His is no parochial godlet but the One whose glory fills the whole earth (Isa. 6:3).

He is the Creator, not a human invention. This conviction was at the heart of Israel's faith: 'My help comes from the LORD, the Maker of heaven and earth' (Ps. 121:2). That is the unbridgeable gap between Yahweh and other gods which are no more than lifeless artefacts. This God listens and once again we remember the contrast in 1 Kings 18 between the God who heard Elijah and the lifeless idol of the priests of Baal. Above all He is the living God who sees and hears all that is in heaven and earth.

Hezekiah's prayer is not for personal vindication but that the world might know that there is no other God. This is the basis for evangelism and the authority to preach the Gospel to every nation because there is no other god who can save (see Acts 4:12). Sennacherib and his gods had defeated and humiliated the other nations and their gods but he had not met the true God.

Isaiah's powerful words (19:20-34)

Back in 18:20 the Rabshakeh had said that Hezekiah had spoken 'empty words' but now here are words which create and destroy, 'This is the Word that the LORD has spoken.' The words of the LORD through Isaiah rather than the boasts of Assyria are to dominate the chapter. This long prophecy bears specifically on this situation but like all true prophecy has a much wider application.

First the ridicule which Sennacherib has directed at Zion is turned back on him. Sennacherib thinks he can despise this city and its king but it is Zion who is mocking him. 'The One enthroned in heaven laughs, the LORD scoffs at them' (Ps. 2:4). It is not in fact the Virgin Daughter of Zion whom the Assyrian has mocked but the Holy One of Israel whose awesome power Isaiah had seen (Isa. 6) and which had marginalised all Sennacherib's boasted pomp and show.

Sennacherib speaks and behaves as if he is a god and his boasts in verses 23-4 are paralleled in his annals and those of other Assyrian kings.[2] Since these are boasts we need not be pedantically literal about their accuracy. He did not literally dry up the streams of Egypt but there is little doubt that he imagined he could if he wanted.[3] This is macho bragging and speaking as if he were invincible.

---

2.   See Davis p.285.

3.   It was in fact his son Esarhaddon (v. 37) who conquered Egypt briefly, an event referred to in Nahum 3:8-10. Yet this was the beginning of Assyria's downfall having stretched herself too far.

Sennacharib believes the whole earth known to him is at his feet and that he controls the whole terrain whether mountain, forest or river.

What he fails to realise is that he is not lord of history not even his own but a mere instrument in the hand of Yahweh who is carrying out His judgments in the earth. Long before Sennacherib's time, Yahweh had planned for the Assyrian to be the rod of His anger (Isa. 10:5) and then for that rod itself to be broken. They would suffer the same fate they inflicted on their prisoners and dragged with hooks away to exile. Sennacherib, like 'a poor player, struts and frets his hour upon the stage and then is heard no more.'[4]

But what will happen to Judah once the Assyrians have left? The devastated land will recover within two years (vv. 29-31). By the third year normal agricultural practice will resume. This will also be true spiritually as a remnant will remain through whom God's promises will be carried out. This will be carried out by 'the zeal' of the LORD, and Isaiah points to how this will be done by a unique son of David who will reign forever (Isa. 9:6-7).

Meanwhile, the city of David will be saved (vv. 32-34). This will happen before Sennacherib can prepare for the final onslaught on the city. Sadly, in a later generation, Jeremiah had to warn that taking this promise for granted while despising the commands of Yahweh would lead to disaster.

The judgment on Assyria and its king (19:35-37)
With terrifying swiftness, the judgment on Assyria unfolds and the invincible army fades away. The agent of that

---

4.   William Shakespeare, *Macbeth*. Act 5. Sc. 5.24-5.

judgment is the angel of Yahweh who had passed through Egypt (Exod. 12:12) and who had come between the fleeing Israelites and the pursuing Egyptians (Exod. 14:19). Sennacherib has to beat an ignominious retreat with what remains of his army. The psalmist exults that Zion is still there and her ramparts and citadels are intact (Ps. 48:13). In a similar vein, Psalm 46:5 speaks of the city which is secure because God is within her.

This account has attracted widespread scepticism with many regarding it as a pious legend but that is a product of rationalism rather than evidence from the text. The most important outside clue is that Sennacherib, having lavishly portrayed the fall of Lachish, does not mention the capture of Jerusalem. It is inconceivable that if Jerusalem had been taken he would not have recorded it and boasted about it. The Assyrian spin doctors did not record failures.

A number of years passed between verses 34 and 35 but Sennacherib is history. Hezekiah had spread the letter before Yahweh but the Assyrian god proves as impotent as his master and cannot protect him. Goliath has once again been defeated by David's God. The prophecy of Isaiah in verse 7 is fulfilled as Adrammelech and Sharezer commit patricide and Sennacherib bleeds out on the floor of the temple of his nation's godlet.

From text to message

Getting the message clear: the theme
The words of Psalm 46:7, 'The LORD of hosts is with us, the God of Jacob is our fortress', have already been noted as possibly referring to the events of this chapter. In any case what happens here is a perfect illustration of this truth.

The Lord saves and vindicates His people and this is the basis of our faith.

Getting the message clear: the aim

This passage is a powerful demonstration of how we need to have big ideas of God to help us to pray to Him in times of crisis. The aim is to link our helplessness with the power of God and fill us with great ideas of God to help us to pray to Him in times of crisis. The aim is to link our helplessness with the power of God. A good text to introduce this is Proverbs 21:30, 'There is no wisdom, no insight, no plan that can succeed against the LORD.'

A way in

Perhaps speaking about the Assyrian rooms in the British Museum as mentioned at the beginning of the exposition would be useful. First of all it would show we are dealing with real events in history not pious legends. Also it is an important reminder that God is not simply concerned about our personal lives but is active at the great moments in history. Indeed, it is because of that that we can trust Him with our little lives. The fact that He can deal with Sennacherib means that He can handle the Islamic state, the drug barons and the war lords. Thus, we can also call on Him in unemployment, in cancer and in bereavement.

Ideas for application

+   In a world and indeed a church where we are often inclined to depend on our strengths we need to be reminded that we are weak and vulnerable and that often our resources will run out.

+   Hezekiah's prayer (vv. 15-19) is a model of true prayer because it springs from a conviction about who God is and that He will listen and answer. Even so-called 'arrow prayers' where we simply call out for help must be based on a true theology of God.

+   The importance of the prophetic Word is emphasised again and is in contrast to arrogant boasting. The conviction here is that God listens to one 'who is humble and contrite in spirit and who trembles at my Word'.

+   The theology of history shows we can endure in tough times; even when the world seems out of control God is in charge. This is the importance of the doctrine of providence, not as an abstraction but as an encouragement that our labour 'is not in vain in the Lord' (1 Cor. 15:58).

+   The concern of God for the practicalities of daily living in Isaiah's words about how agriculture will return to normal within three years shows that He is not simply concerned with the removal of the Assyrian threat but about life returning to normal. The Lord cares about our homes and families, our work and leisure and we need to thank Him for that more than we do.

+   This story is a powerful warning against pride and its deadly consequences. This applies to God's people as well. Reflect on the chilling words used about King Uzziah, 'he was marvellously helped until he became strong' (2 Chron. 26:15).

Suggestions for preaching

Sermon 1
We could preach the chapter as a whole using similar titles to those suggested at the beginning of the exposition.

An urgent plea (19:1-13)
The king sends to the prophet recognising he needs his help.

A powerful prayer (19:14-19)
Emphasising the God to whom we pray.

An authoritative prophecy (19:20-35)
Words of God dismissing the Assyrian boasts and first humiliating and then destroying Sennacherib.

Sermon 2
Another approach would be to take Hezekiah's prayer (19:14-19) and use this to comment on the whole story; A title like 'God's power made perfect in human weakness' would be suitable.

The God who hears

The God who is on the throne

The God who is the Creator

The God whose glory fills the earth

Sermon 3
Could take the whole passage from 18:17 to 19:35 and preach a similar sermon to sermon 1 – you would need to be selective.

Suggestions for teaching

Questions to help understand the passage

1. Why does Hezekiah tear his clothes and put on sackcloth (v. 10)?

2. Why does Hezekiah say 'It may be'? (v. 4)

3. What shows Isaiah's confidence?

4. Why are verses 10ff repeated from 18:34ff?

5. Why does Hezekiah go to the temple and spread the letter before the LORD? (v. 14)

6. What kind of God does Hezekiah believe in?

7. In what way has Sennacherib insulted Yahweh?

8. What implicit claims is Sennacherib making in verses 23-4?

9. What do verses 25-6 show about what happens in history?

10. Why are verses 29-31 important?

11. Why is David mentioned? (v. 34)

12. What does verse 37 show about the Assyrian gods?

Questions to help apply the passage

1. What do verses 1-4 show about Hezekiah's faith in the prophetic Word? Remember he had a channel built to bring water into Jerusalem in the event of a siege. What does this show about his priorities?

2. Why do verses 5-7 still mean that faith is necessary?

3. What is Sennacherib's theology of the gods (vv. 10-13)? What kind of attitudes reflect that today?

4. Hezekiah got rid of external props to faith, including the bronze serpent (18:4). Why does he go to the Temple?

5. What lessons about effective prayer do we learn from verses 14-19?

6. What does verse 20 show about the access of the true prophet to God? How does this help us to discern the true voice of God today?

7. There is a powerful analysis of pride in this story but we must not think ourselves immune. Read and reflect on Genesis 3:6 and 1 John 2:15-17 and see how pride is the natural human condition without the grace of God.

8. What is the significance of the 'remnant'? (vv. 30-1)

9. What does verse 34 tell us about the importance of the covenant with David? See 2 Samuel 7 and think about the promise there is to be fulfilled.

10. How does verse 35 recall the Exodus story and thus link this with the heart of Israel's faith?

11. Why is Sennacherib dismissed so summarily, how does this reinforce the overall significance of the story and also make a devastating comment on idolatry?

17

GRACE FROM START TO FINISH (20)

Introduction

There is a certain type of Christian biography, perhaps better hagiography, which presents its subject as attaining a level of almost perfection that leaves us struggling with our temptations and besetting sins wondering if we are Christian at all. How gratefully we turn to the Bible where the One who knows the secrets of our hearts presents faithful and unbiased pictures of the people of faith. Hezekiah, for all his faith, had flaws and in this chapter is shown in all his weakness and vulnerability and yet the final assessment does not contradict the picture of chapters 18 and 19.

Here Hezekiah is in two situations which in different ways put him at risk and threaten his wellbeing. The first is a life-threatening illness which again shows him at prayer and receiving the prophetic Word. The story of his healing and the method used is full of interest. The second is a major attack on his faith this time not from militarism but from flattery and the temptation to be seen as a big player on the international scene. The final verses, however, round off his story in a favourable and positive way.

Above all it is a story of God's grace, 'grace to cover all my sin'.[1] The best of the kings only make it by grace. That needs to be our focus as we preach on this passage, otherwise we will be in danger of a moralising rant which magnifies Hezekiah's flaws and minimises our own.

Listening to the text

Context and structure

At a hasty reading we might imagine that the incidents of this chapter follow chronologically from chapters 18 and 19 but verse 6 sees the rescue of Jerusalem as still future. The clue is in the two phrases, 'in those days' (v. 1) and 'at that time' (v. 12) which are common narrative devices indicating that these events happened in the reign of Hezekiah but not dating them precisely. Often Biblical narrative, like other narrative, will adopt an arrangement of events which is not chronological. We noticed that this is probably the case in the Elisha stories. At the end of 2 Samuel, chapters 21-4, go back to earlier periods of David's life which show the king in various capacities as psalmist, warrior and shepherd of his people.

The question is why this chapter (and Isaiah 38 and 39) are here. The reason is the words of Isaiah (vv. 16-18) which tell of the inevitability of exile, not in Assyria but in Babylon. Many good things, notably the reforms of Josiah, are still to happen but Judah will eventually go the same

---

1.   From Charles Wesley, 'Jesus, Lover of my soul'.

way as Israel. The final assessment of Hezekiah, as of later Josiah, is positive but still neither could prevent the Exile.

There are two main sections in the chapter as well as a footnote assessing Hezekiah's reign.

+ Grace which responds to faith (20:1-11)

+ Grace which is not turned away by failure (20:12-19)

+ Grace in the final assessment (20:20-21)

Working through the text

Grace which responds to faith (20:1-11)
It all seems so unfair that this godly and capable king is about to be taken away from the people he served so faithfully and the reforms he so vigorously implemented. Thus the prophet's words are grim and the future is bleak. Hezekiah responds to the prospect of death as he is to respond to the threats of Sennacherib, he turns to prayer.

Some have been critical of his prayer and compared it unfavourably to 19:15-19 where his concern is for God's glory whereas here it appears to be self-centred.[2] However, it is possible to read the prayer in quite a different way. First the king takes the prophet's words not as final but as a challenge to pray. Hezkiah is not claiming to be perfect, but he is saying he has walked in faithfulness. This most Davidic of kings lays hold of some of the promises in the Davidic psalms, for example 18:20-4, where David speaks of Yahweh honouring his righteousness and clean hands. This is claiming covenant promises before the covenant Lord who honours those promises.

---

2. E.g. Provan p.263.

The main reason, though, for seeing this prayer as honouring the Lord is that the Lord answers. Yahweh accepts Hezekiah's plea by calling him 'the leader of my people' (v. 5), and sends Isaiah back with a different message. Again, Isaiah emphasises the link with David which is important throughout the story. Yahweh again reveals the kind of God He is: One who listens and sympathises. He deals first with the immediate situation, 'I will heal you', but goes far beyond the request and promises fifteen years of life and rescue from Assyria. This is the God 'who is able to do immeasurably more than all we ask or imagine' (Eph. 3:20)

The answer is followed by healing and a sign. God heals but He uses means, in this case a poultice of figs, apparently a common practice.[3] The sign plainly was asked for before the healing. This is reflected in the NIV's translation of verse 8: 'Hezekiah *had* asked'. The actual details of the sign are not totally clear; but the sign was for Hezekiah and not for us. Perhaps the 'steps' referred to the gradations on a sundial but they may have just as well been literal steps constructed by Ahaz on which the sunlight fell indicating various times of day. Just as the shadow disappeared as the sun rose higher, so now the shadow of death which had hung over Hezekiah would disappear for fifteen years. In any case both the sign and the prolonging of life were actions of the living God.

Grace which is not turned away by failure (12:12-19)
A very different scenario and a very different kind of danger now presents itself. A visit from some distinguished messengers come from Merodach Baladan of Babylon.

---

3.   One such commentator is Provan, p. 263.

Hezekiah was human; it must have been flattering to receive such important visitors and to be seen as a big player on the international stage. Merodach Baladan was concerned that Hezekiah was ill and even sent a get-well letter and a present! The temptation of a seat at the top table was too much for Hezekiah to resist. Hezekiah, like many another, was to prove a stalwart at standing up to bullies but was swept off his feet by flattery.

But into this scene comes the prophet with a Word of judgment. His question about the identity of the visitors is not probably because he did not know who they were but rather to get Hezekiah to see the reality of the situation. A question like 'Adam, where are you?' (Gen. 3:9), which heralds a judgment from God. Exile is coming and neither people nor possessions will remain.

Hezekiah's response (v. 19) has been scrutinised as a selfish, cynical comment, something along the lines of 'Well, at least it won't happen on my watch', but again it can be read totally differently. Hezekiah first acknowledges that the Word of God is good. There is mercy as well as judgment and Hezekiah will be spared from exile as Josiah is also to be spared. In any case even the godly are only saved by grace and God's judgments are never excessive.

Grace in the final assessment of Hezekiah (20:20-21)
So what is the final verdict on this flawed but faithful king? We need to take the 'bookends' of the story, these verses along with 18:1-8 which present a thoroughly positive picture of his achievements. Special mention is made of his bringing water into the city running from the Gihon spring to provide amidst a possible siege (see 2 Chron. 32:2-4). Mention has already been made of Psalm 46:4, 'There is a

river whose streams make glad the city of God' and while
the ultimate reference is to the heavenly Jerusalem there
may be a hint of this earthly stream which provided water
at a time of danger.

He was buried in the royal tombs (2 Chron. 32:33)
leaving an honoured name and a reflection of the great days
of David. This was soon to be challenged and disaster is
soon to strike.

From text to message

Getting the message clear: the theme
This chapter is about the need of grace in every circumstance
of life whether apparently disastrous or apparently
favourable. Even the best of us are weak and need grace
from start to finish.

Getting the message clear: the aim
The need to see beyond the outward and discern what the
Lord is saying in every circumstance of life.

A way in
We need to be realistic in our expectations of our leaders.
God is faithful but leaders are flawed. That does not mean
denigrating good leaders but it does mean not expecting
them to be flawless. It is God's work and while we can
never serve Him perfectly, by His grace we can serve Him
acceptably.

Ideas for application
+   We cannot expect that faithfulness to God will shield
     us from illness and other traumas. The book of Job is
     a useful corrective to such ideas but throughout the

Bible God's people suffer the same troubles as others, and illnesses like depression are as prevalent among Christians as among the general population.

+ Prayer often challenges God and this is a common feature of many of the Psalms and the book of Jeremiah.

+ The prophetic Word is a constant need as we try to understand the perplexities of life.

+ We need to be aware of the danger of flattery. This was not just a problem for the king of Judah. We love to 'name drop' and often to claim a closer friendship with the gurus than we have. Think of this. When you stand in glory and see someone who was a big name on earth, he is there for exactly the same reason as you, a sinner saved by grace.

+ The assessment of any of our lives is only provisional in this world and the final verdict will be one which is given by the Lord, the righteous Judge.

Suggestions for preaching

We might want to use the suggested outline with two main points and the last two verses as a kind of footnote. The emphasis would be on grace, on the God who understands and cares and on the flawed but faithful servant. A similar outline might be:

+ Trusting God in danger (vv. 1-11) – the blend of prayer and the prophetic Word.

+ Wobbling because of flattery (vv. 12-19) – a lapse but still trusting in God's good purposes.

✦   A divine assessment (vv. 20-1) – the Davidic king has
    been a true shepherd to his people.

Suggestions for teaching

Questions to help understand the passage

1. What are the implications of the phrase 'in those
    days'? (v. 1)

2. Is Hezekiah being conceited and self-centred? (v. 3)

3. Why does he ask for a sign? (v. 8)

4. Why does Hezekiah show such attention to the
    messengers from Babylon? (v. 13)

5. How does Isaiah's message (vv. 16-18) blend
    judgment and mercy?

6. Why does Hezekiah say the Word is 'good'? (v. 19)

7. What is the author's final assessment of Hezekiah?
    (vv. 20-21) You might want to read again 18:1-8.

Questions to help apply the passage

1. What is our natural reaction on reading verse 1?
    What does this say about our ideas of fairness?

2. What important lessons about prayer are shown in
    v. 3? Why do we need to learn these?

3. What kind of a God is Yahweh shown to be in
    verse 5? It would be useful to read Exodus 34:6-7
    for the picture of God which was at the heart of
    Israel's faith.

4. What does the sign, although the details are not entirely clear, show about God and His control of time? Does this relate to the fifteen extra years promised to Hezekiah?

5. Why does Hezekiah succumb to flattery? How can we recognise and avoid this?

6. What does verse 19 show about accepting the will of God?

7. What do verses 20-1 show about the correct assessment of people's lives and ministries? How can we avoid excessive adulation and excessive criticism?

18

Judah's Ahab (21)

Introduction

It is difficult to imagine a stronger condemnation of a king of Judah than to be compared to 'Ahab king of Israel'. Here the kingdom of Judah after the faithful if flawed Hezekiah is plunged into a darkness and paganism worse than that under Ahaz (chapter 16). For almost sixty years the kingdom becomes the scene of undiluted idolatry.[1] This was no unfortunate lapse but a deliberate and systematic dismantling of the reforms of Hezekiah. The advances of one generation can so easily be lost by the next.

The chapter does not have the strong narrative drive of the Hezekiah story and indeed reads like a judicial verdict. This is in fact what it is as the Judge of all the earth gives His verdict on these miserable years. It is a warning story of the

---

1. There is a problem with chronology here which is probably best solved by assuming that Manasseh was co-regent with his father for a decade and that his fifty-five year reign includes that earlier period. See Davis p.302.

danger of 'a sinful and unbelieving heart which turns away from the living God.' (Heb. 3:12). This, the longest reign of any king of Judah, or for that matter, Israel, plumbed new depths of apostasy.

Listening to the text

Context and structure

The chronology as noted is rather puzzling but the real mystery here is why God permitted this man to reign for so long. This is often the case in the history of the church and at such times we need to trust the providence of God and realise He is still in control and that in His time He will intervene. Probably we can see Manasseh's reign as part of God's judgment on the people who (v. 11) were complicit in his godlessness. In the flow of the story this chapter is a dark contrast to Hezekiah and Josiah and is therefore a warning against complacency.

There are four main sections:

+ Turning his back on Yahweh (21:1-9)

+ Judgment of God (21:10-15)

+ Corrupting the nation's life (21:16-18)

+ A dismal legacy (21:19-26)

Working through the text

Turning his back on Yahweh (21:1-9)

No reason is given for Manasseh's godlessness and some have suggested that there was probably an anti-Hezekiah party who had opposed the king's reforms and bided their time. That may be but it is speculation; what is evident is that godliness is not transmitted through the genes. What occurs here is no carelessness or weakness but a deliberate attempt to destroy his father's legacy.

This amounts to a systematic determination to turn the clock back not just to the idolatry of his grandfather Ahaz but to the paganism of the early Canaanite nations. Notice the number of references to Yahweh (vv. 2, 4, 5, 6, 7, 9), the covenant Lord. Manasseh is not simply disobeying this or that law but rejecting any relationship with the Lord, deliberately turning his back and turning his heart away from Yahweh. Thus, he restores the high places with all their associations to fertility rites and pagan worship. Worse still, he makes an Asherah pole 'as Ahab king of Israel had done,' (v. 3) the symbol of the fertility goddess and as an ultimate insult places it in the Temple as if she were Yahweh's consort. This is not only taking a mistress but having her live in the marital home. Manasseh's Judah now is the mirror image of Ahab's Israel. To this paganism Manasseh adds the appalling and unnatural cruelty of child sacrifice and dabbles in the dark arts. Twice (vv. 2 and 6) we are told Manasseh did evil in the eyes of Yahweh and thus provoked His righteous anger.

This is no mere random list of Manasseh's sins and corrupt practices, behind it is a total rejection of the revelation God had given to His people; hence the reference to Moses (v. 8). Manasseh rejected the God of the Exodus (v. 2) and turned his back on the whole history of the Lord's protection of His people. He rejected the God of Creation who 'also made the stars' (Gen. 1:16) and worshipped the creation (v. 5) rather than the Creator. He saw the temple as his own private chapel in which he could erect altars to any god or goddess he wanted. He despised Yahweh's promises, Yahweh's temple, Yahweh's land and Yahweh's Word and duped the nation into following him into occultic, brutal, retrogressive paganism. Manassah, as leader, was most responsible but he had the consent of at least the majority.

Judgment of God (21:10-15)

Yet there were still some faithful voices of prophets underlining and applying the words of Moses. This has been a feature of this book as prophets known and unknown have faithfully spoken to God's true worldly authority. The author not only says that Manasseh was the worst of the kings of Judah but that his evil exceeded that of the Amorites, the pre-Conquest inhabitants of Canaan. A similar comment is made about Ahab (1 Kings 21:26). Ezekiel speaks of apostate Judah under the allegorical name Oholibah and speaks of her depravity in colourful language (Ezek. 23:13-34).

God's judgment is announced in four pictures. The terror inspired by coming judgment is described as making ears 'tingle' (v. 12). In 1 Samuel 3:11, the Lord says that the coming judgment on Eli's house will cause this reaction, and Jeremiah 19:3 uses the Word in relation to the coming Exile. Habbakuk 3:16, also referring to the Babylonian invasion, uses the same Word which is usually translated there as 'quiver'. People may not have trembled at the Word of Moses and the prophets but when disaster comes they certainly will.

The second picture is of the plumb-line which had already measured Ahab and Samaria and found them wanting. Isaiah had used this image of the destruction of Edom (Isa. 34) and Amos of the downfall of Samaria (Amos 7:7-8). Lamentations 2:8 uses the image when Jerusalem has fallen. The plumb-line here and in the other examples shows that the Exile is to be no accident of history but a deliberate and fair judgment of the Lord who rules in the kingdoms of the world and carries out His purpose.

The third picture takes us to the kitchen and the cleaning of dishes after a meal. Jeremiah uses a similar image of Nebuchadnezzar making Jerusalem 'an empty jar' and swallowing the people as a snake does (Jer. 51:34). The image is of total destruction and removal of the people as if they had never been. The fourth picture of God handing the people to their enemies shows how this will happen. Manasseh was simply the most recent and worst example of the apostasy which had marked the people since their ancestors had left Egypt.

Corrupting the nation's life (21:16-18)
A wholesale abandoning of the truth always has consequences in behaviour and lifestyle. Here we learn of Manasseh's bloodthirstiness and cruelty (v. 16). This is another echo of Ahab, the judgment on whose house is to 'avenge the blood of my servants the prophets' (2 Kings 9:7). Isaiah is said to have been one of those murdered by being sawn in two (perhaps referred to in Heb. 11:37). But this was a bloodbath and we may safely assume that a man who had his own son murdered would have no qualms at liquidating opponents.

Moreover, Manasseh was not only Judah's Ahab, but Judah's Jeroboam son of Nebat (1 Kings 12-14) who led Israel into sin and whose bad example is frequently mentioned thereafter. Hezekiah was remembered for his 'achievements', Manasseh is remembered for his sin and leading others into sin. This is what his story was about and it is a dreadful one.

His dismal legacy (21:19-26)

There is no mention here of Manasseh's repentance and subsequent attempts to undo at least some of the damage he had done after the Assyrians took him off to Babylon (2 Chron. 33:11-20). This was probably late in his reign when the significant damage had already been done. Also the reforms were not major like Hezekiah's and appear to have been confined to Jerusalem.[2] It is, of course, good that Manasseh repented but we need to remember that a late repentance, while personally wonderful, does not undo on earth the damage that has been done.

In any case, it made no impression on his son Amon who followed in his father's ways; another reason for supposing Manasseh's change of heart came late in his reign. Also this was no mere copying of his father but his own deliberate choice, 'He forsook the LORD, the God of his fathers' (v. 22). Amon is a shadowy figure and we are not told why his officials assassinated him. Nor do we know who 'the people of the land' were. None of that is of great importance.

What is of great importance is that we feel the exile must happen now and that we will go on to read of the end of Judah as we read of the end of Israel (17:1-6; 18:9-11). Yet at this dark moment, the Lord is still in control and a light shines as we read the last name in the chapter, Josiah who is to reverse Manasseh's sin.

---

2.   For a full discussion see Brian Kelly, 'Manasseh in the Books of Kings and Chronicles' (2 Kings 21:1-18; 2 Chron. 33:1-20) in *Windows into Old Testament History* (Grand Rapids:Eerdmans, 2002) pp. 131-146.

From text to message

Getting the message clear: the theme

We must never underestimate the damage done by deliberate disobedience and the effect this will have on future generations.

Getting the message clear: the aim

To show that the advances made by one generation can be destroyed by the next and thus the need for continual vigilance.

A way in

Think of the mystery of God's ways and how churches and individuals who were once staunch for the Gospel have turned away and not only abandoned the truth but in some case deliberately set out to destroy it.

Ideas for application

* A story like this warns us not to be complacent. A church is only ever one generation away from apostasy.

* Faith is not carried in the genes and godly parentage does not guarantee believing children.

* Danger of reviving old heresies under the guise of new ideas.

* Abandoning confidence in the Word of God will eventually lead to a corrupt lifestyle. The history of the last two hundred or so years in Theology Faculties and Seminaries illustrates this. It was once believed that we could abandon the Gospel doctrine and keep the

Gospel lifestyle; recent decades have shown this is not possible.

✦   The dismal legacy of Manasseh shows that unbelief influences future generations. Francis Schaeffer, whose ministry in apologetics was so blessed in the twentieth century, said that we must ask of any teaching what effect it would have on our grandchildren. In the note of hope which ends this chapter we may be glad that one grandchild did not follow the ways of his grandfather.

Suggestions for preaching

We might use a title like 'Playing with fire' echoing Hebrews 12:29, 'Our God is a consuming fire'. In the introduction we could point out that this chapter is a necessary warning against complacency and idolatry. We could then make three main points.

Deliberate unfaithfulness (21:1-9)
Not a lapse but rejection of covenant relationship and dismantling of Hezekiah's reforms. Manasseh's Judah is like Ahab's Israel.

Devastating judgment (21:10-16)
Powerful pictures of judgment and the bloodthirsty consequences of idolatry.

Dismal legacy (21:17-26)
Manasseh is remembered for his sin – Amon followed him but chose this way.

Note of hope – Josiah.

Suggestions for teaching

Questions to help understand the passage

1. Why are the ancient nations of Canaan mentioned? (v. 2)

2. What does verse 3 suggest about Manasseh's attitude to his father?

3. Why is Ahab mentioned? (v. 3)

4. What was so offensive about the Asherah pole?

5. What does verse 6 show about Manasseh's worldview?

6. Why is Moses mentioned? (v. 8)

7. How do we know that Manasseh's activities are the logical outcome of centuries of apostasy?

8. What is striking about Manasseh's obituary? (v. 17)

9. How do we know that Amon was not simply following his father?

10. Can we find any hope in this chapter? Look at verse 26c.

Questions to help apply the passage

1. What do we learn in verse 1 about the mystery of God's ways? Providence is a vital Biblical doctrine and we need to believe it firmly especially at a time like this.

2. Old heresies often masquerade as new insights. Think about contemporary examples.

3. How do verses 7 and 8 show us that we cannot simply disregard various parts of the Bible but when we turn from God's Word the whole Gospel unravels?

4. What does verse 9 show us about bad leadership and its effects on those led?

5. Read 2 Chronicles 33. Can we reconcile the Kings and Chronicles accounts and what lessons do we learn from both?

19

God's Unexpected Intervention (22)

Introduction

When the boy Josiah came to the throne there would have been very few people alive who would remember the reforms of his great grandfather Hezekiah now many decades in the past. These reforms had been systematically dismantled by his grandfather Manasseh, and his father Amon had continued the downward slide. Now the reformation is to burst into life again and instead of immediate exile as we might have expected after chapter 21 an even more comprehensive programme of reforms is launched.

Here we have God's unexpected intervention and a powerful reminder that the Lord can and sometimes does do something new when all that had been expected is decline. For those (and there would be some) who had mourned the godlessness of Zion this was like streams in the desert.

Listening to the text

Context and structure

As already noted we would have expected the exile to come and the end of Judah as a kingdom, instead what happens is the most sustained and comprehensive reformation undertaken by any king. The obvious question is why has this happened now? In one sense this is again the mystery of God's providence. However, when we come across a work of God which seems to come from nowhere, when we dig more deeply we see signs of God working behind the scenes and preparing the ground.

When we look at Josiah's early life we realise that a number of prophets had been active. Josiah came to the throne in 640 B.C. at a time when Assyria, while still powerful, will soon be crushed by the rising power of Babylon and Nineveh was to fall in 612 B.C. Nahum prophesies Assyria's downfall but begins his prophecy with a powerful hymn (1:2-8) which speaks of the God of the Exodus and His control of creation and history. Habakkuk speaks of Babylon's rise and ultimate fall and the abuses he speaks of in 1:2-4 and again in chapter 2 strongly suggest a date in Manasseh's reign. But perhaps the most significant influence was Zephaniah whose lengthy genealogy at the beginning of his book (1:1) contains the name Hezekiah. This is probably the great reforming king and Zephaniah may even have been Josiah's cousin. The abuses mentioned in his first chapter are exactly those practised by Manasseh which Josiah is to get rid of.[1] This story is to strengthen and build up faith and expectation.

---

1.   There has been a lot of speculation about Josiah's relationship or lack of it with Jeremiah whose ministry began some five years before the

We can divide the chapter into four sections:

✦   A faithful king (22:1-2)

✦   The work on the Temple (22:3-7)

✦   The discovery of the Book of the Law (22:8-13)

✦   The prophecy of Huldah (22:14-20)

Working through the text

A faithful king (22:1-2)
As with Hezekiah, a light shines in the darkness and another king does 'right in the eyes of the LORD' and walks 'in all the ways of his father David'. As a boy of eight it would inevitably be some years before he was able to establish the direction of the kingdom. The Chronicler tells us that at the age of sixteen 'he began to seek the God of his father David' and four years later launched his great reformation. (2 Chron. 34:3)

One further detail is added, and this is not said of any other king of Judah, 'not turning aside to the right or to the left' (v. 2). This refers to Deuteronomy 17:20 where Moses says that a king is to write the words of the law and to make this his lifelong reading. There is also the echo of 1 Kings 2:3-4, the words of David to Solomon which we identified as the key to understanding the whole book. Manasseh and Amon's idolatry is to be swept aside.

---

king came to the throne. There is not enough evidence to be certain but a careful reading of Jeremiah 22:15-16 where the prophet rebukes Jehoiakim for his betrayal of his father Josiah's legacy shows that Josiah's reign was a genuine picture of the king who was to come.

The work on the Temple (22:3-7)
This early work on the Temple initially recalls that of
the earlier king Joash (chapter 12) but the outcome is
very different. Presumably Shaphan had been Josiah's
mentor during his minority and now carries out the king's
wishes. There is far more detail in 2 Chronicles 35 about
temple issues whereas Josiah's reforms in the next chapter
(chapter 23) are to focus on the undoing of Manasseh's
idolatry. Once again a different emphasis does not imply
inconsistency or contradiction. The industry and honesty
of the temple officials in financial matters are emphasised.

The Discovery of the Book of the Law (22:8-13)
But these early reforms are overshadowed by the discovery
of the Book of the Law. The text is emphatic, 'the Book of
the Law I have found'. What was this book and why had it
been lost? It was almost certainly the book of Deuteronomy
the basic covenant document. Liberal scholarship has
argued that while at least some of Deuteronomy may go
back to Moses, the book was actually a product of a group
of reformers who used Moses' name to lend authority to
their views and that it was 'found' just at the right time in
the Temple. The problem with this view, apart from the lack
of anything that can reasonably be called evidence, is that
it was clearly known to David (1 Kings 2:2-4) and to the
reforming kings such as Asa, Jehoshaphat and Hezekiah.

Certainly the reforms had already begun before the
discovery of the book but we need to remember the
influence of Zephaniah and the fact that what we have in
Kings is a thematic rather than chronological account of
Josiah's reign. The overwhelming probability is that the
book had been deliberately suppressed by Manasseh and

allowed to gather dust in some storage cupboard in a dark corner.

Josiah receives the book with deep and heartfelt repentance and sees immediately that the neglect of and disobedience to the Word of God had resulted in judgment. Like all who genuinely respond to the Bible he wants to know more and to plan his future actions accordingly. Thus he sends a delegation to find out exactly what Yahweh is saying for that time.

The Prophecy of Huldah (22:14-20)

At first sight it seems surprising that the officials go to the otherwise unknown Huldah[2] rather than say Zephaniah or Jeremiah. But there is a salutary lesson here. The Book of the Law was the Word of God through Moses and, as has often been noted in this study, there is no authority in the Old Testament which bypasses or supersedes that of Moses. What they were looking for was not another Word which would modify what they had read in the book but for an authentic interpreter who would apply it faithfully to their times. Surely that is what we try to do when we preach and teach the Bible. Also there can be a kind of snobbery that God can or even worse ought to speak only through those whom we know. Always it is the message and not the messenger which is important.

Her message is clear and uncompromising. It is worth noticing first the two ways in which she refers to Josiah. 'Tell the man who sent you' (v. 15) shows the authority with which she speaks. Kings as well as commoners need

---

2. It is possible that Huldah's husband Shallum may have been Jeremiah's uncle (Jer. 32:7) but this is uncertain and nothing is made of it.

to hear and tremble; the ground is level before the Word. Then in verse 18 'tell the king of Judah,' which shows her respect for him as the Davidic king and as a true leader who will obey the Word of God whatever it costs.

In true prophetic manner there are two sides to her message. There is a Word of judgment (vv. 16-17). The idolatry and faithlessness to the covenant will be punished and there will be no reprieve. There is a Word of mercy (vv. 18-20) for the king who has repented and sought to obey the Lord.

From text to message

Getting the message clear: the theme
God is still on the throne and can revive His people when He chooses. He moves in mysterious ways but always uses His Word to stir up hearts and change lives.

Getting the message clear: the aim
To encourage us to believe in a God who can intervene and change everything when all hope seems lost.

A way in
It would be encouraging to talk about times when after prolonged departure from the Gospel, God suddenly revives His work. One such time was in the eighteenth century when after many decades of spiritual drought the Lord laid His hand on the Wesleys and Whitfield and a time of great spiritual blessing followed. Further it is vital to remember that all through the times of dryness faithful people prayed and unknown and unsung pastors struggled faithfully in lonely and depressing situations.

Ideas for application

- We need to develop the right kind of expectancy. We never know what God may be about to do. In recent decades there has been a renewed and welcome emphasis on training. How often do we pray for the Lord to raise up Josiahs?

- The importance of 'not turning aside to the right or the left' is still an important issue. Turning to the right can be seen as the way of legalism where the Word is not regarded as sufficient but a whole cluster of non-Biblical rules are added which become as important and eventually more important than the Gospel. Turning to the left can be seen as the way of liberalism where the Word is diminished and other things set the agenda. Both deny the sufficiency of the Word.

- The Word of God is the driving force for every genuine reformation. The book discovered here was not a new invention but the rediscovery of the living Word which had been suppressed for decades. There is no saying what may happen when that Word is unleashed.

- It is not enough to read the Word; there must be a response of repentance and faith.

- God is not confined to working through those we know. Huldah is not known outside this story but her words are powerful and her influence profound.

- Huldah's response to Josiah shows a blend of boldness and respect. She is not overawed by him nor does she grovel. Leaders who are godly deserve respect but they are also fallible humans who need to tremble before the Word of God.

Suggestions for preaching

We can follow the flow of the story under some such title as 'God's unexpected intervention' or 'Light shines into the darkness'.

The introduction would place Josiah briefly in context both historically and canonically, i.e. the background of prophetic activity. Three main points could be made.

Unexpected Grace (22:1-10)
Early and consistent discipleship – Davidic king who restores Word. Work begins on Temple.

Uninhibited Repentance (22:11-13)
Josiah exemplifies the person who 'is humble and contrite in spirit and trembles at the Lord's Word' (Isa. 66:2) – does not stand on his dignity and wants to inquire further.

Uncompromising Clarity (22:14-20)
Moses and the prophets speak with one voice: Word of judgment and a Word of mercy.

Suggestions for teaching

Questions to help understand the passage

1. What is the significance of mentioning that Josiah did not turn to the right or the left? (v. 2)

2. What was the Book of the Law and why had it been lost?

3. What do you notice about Josiah's reaction to the reading of the book? (vv. 11-13)

4. Why does he send for further comment on what he heard?

5. What gives Huldah's words authority? (v. 15)

6. How does the prophetess show that she is not overawed by the king and yet respects him? Compare verses 15 and 18.

Questions to help apply the passage

1. Josiah begins his reforms even before the Book of the Law is discovered. What might have been the influences on him and do these give us encouragement today?

2. In what ways has the 'Book of the Law' been 'lost' in our society and how can we place it centre stage?

3. How does Josiah's reaction show his true repentance even though he was not personally responsible for the sins of his fathers? (v. 13)

4. How do we know Huldah was a genuine prophetess and how does that help us today when people claim to have prophetic gifts?

5. Leaders deserve loyalty and respect when they lead in the true ways of God. How does Huldah's response to Josiah show she is not afraid of him yet has a true loyalty to him under her overriding loyalty to Yahweh?

20

THE BOOK THAT CHANGED
EVERYTHING (23:1-30)

Introduction

None of us know how the cause of God is going to develop in our lifetime and whether we will see great blessing or experience great disappointment. But what are we to do if we knew that little would happen in our day and that we would come to the end of our ministry without a lot to encourage? Of course we do not know but sometimes we are tempted to wonder if our labours are in vain. This chapter show how faithful Josiah, although he knew that his efforts would not avert the Exile, still goes on and does what is right.

The story is powerful and it is not surprising to read that there was never a king like Josiah (v. 25). It is one of the most inspiring examples in the Bible of obedience which is wholehearted and not driven by pragmatic considerations.

Listening to the text

Context and structure

The chapter flows directly from the finding of the Book of the Law (22:8-13) and describes the reforms which resulted. As already pointed out, the arrangement here is thematic rather than chronological and although the reforms would have taken some considerable time they are presented in a concentrated way which maximises their effect. The king's repentance was not cosmetic; this was a root and branch purging of idolatry.

Yet in many ways, at this late stage in the book there is a deliberate echoing of earlier parts of the story emphasising the unity and coherence of the narrative. Idolatry did not begin with Ahaz and Manasseh and we are reminded of the responsibility of Solomon himself (v. 13), echoing 1 Kings 11:4-8. Further we are reminded of the story of the man of God from Judah (vv. 17-18) and the events of 1 Kings 13 which took place some three hundred years earlier but the Word spoken then is now being fulfilled. The reference to Manasseh and the coming Exile (vv. 26-27) shows us that the story of the Judaean monarchy is nearing its end.

The story develops in six sections:

+   The Covenant renewed (23:1-3)

+   Idolatry destroyed (23:4-20)

+   The Passover celebrated (23:21-23)

+   The king honoured (23:24-25)

+   Exile is inevitable (23:26-27)

+   The end of Josiah's reign (23:28-30)

Working through the text

The Covenant renewed (23:1-3)

It is no accident that before any specific activity is undertaken that there is a Covenant renewal ceremony. All idolatry and apostasy begins not with particular actions but with a break in the covenant relationship between the Lord and His people. The king takes the initiative and this is an essential act of leadership. However, all strata of society are involved and this recalls other great covenant renewals such as Joshua 24:1-27 at Shechem where again the Book of the Law is prominent and 1 Samuel 7:12-13 at Mizpah. These all echo the giving of the law at Sinai.

The reading and responding to the book are emphasised (vv. 2-3), the importance of obeying not perfunctorily but with heart and soul. This is a determination not to turn either to the right or the left but to pursue the path of obedience to the Word of God. Thus it is no surprise that what follows is the most radical set of reforms ever undertaken in Judah.

Idolatry destroyed (23:4-20)

The reforms spread out from the Temple itself to Jerusalem and the rest of Judah and indeed beyond to the former kingdom of Israel. Manasseh's idolatry is systematically purged and idolatrous artefacts literally dumped. At the heart of this was the purifying of worship and the re-establishing of the Temple as the place where Yahweh revealed Himself. Baal-worship (see comments on 1 Kings pp. 246-7) with its appeal to hedonism and supernaturalism without sanctity was at the root of the problem of idolatry. The Asherah pole was an affront to the covenant relationship with Yahweh and needed to go.

The notorious high places, removed by Hezekiah and restored by Manasseh, went the same way as did other idolatrous shrines. Not only were such places destroyed they were 'desecrated' (vv. 8, 10, 13, 19) which meant that all relics of paganism were removed and the sites reverted to ordinary purposes. Child sacrifice and sun worship were banned and the whole paraphernalia of idolatry was as if it had never been. The occult, essentially an attempt to find a kind of revelation which was an alternative to the word was summarily dismissed (v. 24).

Three further points, already referred to in the introduction are worth mentioning. Idolatrous worship is traced back to Solomon and the shrines he had built for his foreign wives (1 Kings 11:7-8). Solomon had introduced wholesale idolatry and although the reforming kings, notably Hezekiah, had removed the high places, yet the unsavoury traditions lingered making it easy for the likes of Ahaz and Manasseh to cash in on them. Idolatry is more easily introduced than removed. How tragic it is that Solomon should be remembered for this centuries later.

The second and more positive reference to earlier times is the reminder of 1 Kings 13 where the reforms of Josiah are foretold. Time does not prevent God's Word happening and the great reformation now confirms that the man of God from Judah spoke truth in spite of his untimely end. It is also a further reminder of the way that Jeroboam had led Israel into sin.

The third point which is also significant for the future is that Josiah extended his reforms into the old northern kingdom and to Bethel where Jeroboam had set up golden calves (1 Kings 12:28-30). Jeroboam not only split the kingdom but also divided the worship by denying Yahweh had placed His name in Jerusalem. But God's intention was to reunite His scattered people and this is outlined clearly in Ezekiel 37:15-28 where the prophet is told to join together two sticks as a symbol of the future uniting of God's people who David will reign over for ever. Josiah thus, although he lived before the full revelation, in this as in so much else showed himself in tune with the mind of the Lord.

The Passover celebrated (23:21-23)
A fuller account is found in 2 Chronicles 35 but this brief notice is full of suggestive themes. It is a recall to a renewed relationship with Yahweh the Covenant Lord and a reminder of the past failures to celebrate this most significant festival of the year celebrating the Exodus and the God who freed them from slavery. This Passover is celebrated in Jerusalem where God had placed His name and where His Temple stood. This was a condemnation of high places and other idolatrous shrines and a testimony to Josiah's faithfulness.

The king honoured (23:24-25)
The accolade given here to Josiah is unstinting in its commendation. Some have found it odd that Hezekiah is also said to have no rivals before or after him (18:5). The point is that neither here nor in chapter 18 is either king said to be perfect. Rather Hezekiah's faith and courage are unparalleled and here it is Josiah's wholehearted obedience to the Word of God which is singled out. This loyalty was no mere pedantic rule keeping, but a desire to shape his life and the nation's life along godly lines. If Hezekiah was the new David, Josiah was the new Moses.

It is no accident that this obedience is linked with getting rid of mediums, spiritists and idols. These were alternative and forbidden sources of guidance and alleged wisdom. A little thought would have shown that trying to find guidance from the dead and dumb idols was foolish, but history proves otherwise.

Exile is inevitable (23:26-27)

Josiah already knew from Huldah that the nation had gone too far, yet he did not slacken the vigorous programme of reform. However, it still comes as a rude shock that even this could not avert judgment. Yet this reformation was not ultimately useless because it showed how faithfulness is still possible and commendable even when there will be no pragmatic results. It is enshrined here in the Bible as an encouragement to be faithful and trust the Lord with the results.

It is plain that Manasseh's belated repentance was far too little far too late and that God knew that even these massive reforms had not fundamentally changed the nation as was to be evident when Josiah was no longer there. Jeremiah is to wrestle long and hard with the problems of God's sovereign choice and equally sovereign rejection.

The end of Josiah's reign (23:28-30)

The last part of this section is sad reading as Josiah's end foreshadows that of Judah. Assyria was weakening, and the Pharaoh, alarmed at the rising power of Babylon, went to help the tottering empire. Josiah, probably to show his independence of Assyria, unwisely intervened and lost his life. This does not contradict Huldah's words (22:20) which said that Josiah would be taken before the Exile but said nothing of how he would die.

He was a truly good king and a light in the darkness. But that darkness is now to descend more deeply and all he did is to be undone. Yet even here there is blessing as Josiah is spared the tragedy of the Exile.

From text to message

Getting the message clear: the theme
The theme is a solemn one: even the most thoroughgoing reformation may come too late. Yet it is still right to trust and obey even if we cannot see any lasting good come from it.

Getting the message clear: the aim
To show that it is always necessary to obey and leave the results to God.

A way in
We need to have a long hard look at the relationship of obedience to success. If we are faithful there will probably be some blessing but sometimes someone may be sent to a place which has rejected the gospel for years and the message is to be one of judgment. We would need to be certain in that case and the message would be of Christ but we know that there will always be some who do not smell a sweet fragrance but the stench of death (2 Cor. 2:16).

Ideas for application
+   Before detailed reforms, Josiah restored the covenant relationship. Unless that happens all we do will be simply programmes and methods.

+   1 John 5:21 says, 'Dear children, keep yourselves from idols'. Often these are obvious as here but it is always easier to see the idolatry of others rather than ourselves. What idols are particular temptations to evangelicals and how can we avoid them?

+ There is another striking example here of the power of God's words long after they are spoken in the reminder of 1 Kings 13. Do we have real confidence in that Word even if its results are not obvious in our lifetime?

+ The Passover not only recalls the Exodus but points forward to the Cross and Resurrection; we need to keep these fresh in our hearts and minds.

+ Josiah could not save his people but his Descendant would and in that we can have hope in the darkest days.

Suggestions for preaching

Sermon 1
Could follow the flow of the narrative with some such title as 'Great but doomed faithfulness'.

Renewing Relationships (1-3)

Removing Hindrances (4-20)

Back to Roots (21-23)

Well done but not the One who is to come (24-30)

Sermon 2
Could adopt a more topical treatment and focus on such themes as:

Godly Leadership

Obeying the Word

Faithfulness in dark days.

Suggestions for Teaching

Questions to help understand the passage

1. How is the importance of the Book of the Law emphasised? (vv. 1-3)

2. Why do the reforms begin with the Temple?

3. What do verses 4-7 show about the nature of idol worship?

4. Why are 'the kings of Judah' (vv. 5, 11) mentioned?

5. What is the point of referring to Solomon? (v. 13)

6. Read 1 Kings 13 and show why it is echoed here. (vv. 16-18)

7. How do verses 21-23 show that Josiah's Passover was central to his reforms?

8. Why mention the occult in verse 24?

9. What do verses 26-27 add to the story?

10. Does Josiah's death in verse 29 contradict 22:20?

Questions to help apply the passage

1. A former king of Israel, Jehu (2 Kings 9 and 10) got rid of Baal worship in Samaria. What were the main differences between him and Josiah? Think about the absence of the mention of the Book of the Law in Jehu's story and the lack of any evidence of real spiritual life in Jehu.

2. 'All his heart and soul' (v. 2). Read chapter 12 and notice the absence of that (and indeed the Book

of the Law) in the story of Joash and the repair of the Temple. Are we afraid of heart and soul involvement? Different people will show this in different ways but it is so easy to run programmes which are long on efficiency and short on prayer.

3. Solomon's legacy was dire and lingered on after his great achievements disappeared. Idolatry remains a massive temptation for all of us. How can we avoid leaving a dangerous example to future generations?

4. What is the significance of the Passover for today?

5. What lessons can we learn from Josiah's leadership?

21

Zion Down but not Out (23:31–25:30)

Introduction

The final section of Kings is about Exile. 'So Judah went into Exile away from her own land' (25:21b). These sad words encapsulate the bleak atmosphere of the last days of Judah. The final days of the kingdom are told briefly and tersely. The story which began with the glory days of Solomon ends with a defeated and humiliated province from which everyone who was anyone and everything which was anything have been carted off to Babylon. Yet that is not quite the end and the apparently irrelevant incident (25:27-30) about the former king of Judah, Jehoiachin, sounds a note of hope. Two introductory comments can be made.

The first is that there is little overt theological comment here. We noticed in the exposition of chapter 17:7-41 that the author in the aftermath of Israel's exile to Assyria takes the opportunity to comment extensively on the disobedience and unbelief which had led to this and that this does double duty for the future exile of Judah. However, the way the narrative unfolds implies its own comments on why these dreadful events were happening. Look again at the remarks on Old Testament narrative (Introduction pp. 47-50). As we shall see the author's selection of material and how he presents it makes its own assessment.

The second is a historical note to help to navigate the events. The time covered is 608 B.C. when Josiah died to 587 or 586 when Jerusalem fell. See Introduction p. 46-52 for the specific dates of the four kings. Internationally Assyria has fallen and the scene is dominated by the rising power of Babylon under Nebuchadnezzar who inflicted a heavy defeat on Pharaoh Neco at Carchemish in Syria (24:7). Thereafter the Exile happens in stages before the final destruction and deportation. The invasion of Judah by Nebuchadnezzar (24:1) is the one in which Daniel and his friends and other youths were taken to Babylon (Dan. 1:1-4) and trained in Babylonian ways. The second deportation (24:10-16) further deprived Judah of leaders and this was the time Ezekiel was deported (Ezek. 1:1-3). Finally (25:11-12), following Zedekiah's rebellion, Jerusalem was besieged and destroyed and the final deportation took place. Two footnotes follow. The first is the setting up of a short-lived provisional government under Gedaliah (25:22-26) and the second some twenty-six years later of Jehoiachin's honourable status in Babylon (25:27-30).

Listening to the text

Context and structure
The link with previous chapters is established in 24:3-4 where we are reminded yet again that what is happening

is an inevitable consequence of Manasseh's apostasy. But also as the story nears its end there is an implied contrast. The united kingdom, with its peace, prosperity and the excitement surrounding the building and dedication of the Temple, is contrasted with the sadness of its destruction. There is then a striking and more immediate contrast between the final kings of Judah and the robust faith of Hezekiah and the reforming zeal of Josiah. Instead we have unbelief, futile politicking and a sense of coming doom. The lights are going out.

There are four main sections:

+ The tarnished crown (23:31-24:20)

+ The fall of Jerusalem (25:1-21)

+ Mayhem and muddle (25:22-26)

+ Long live the king (25:27-30)

Working through the text

The tarnished crown (23:31-24:20)

It has already been made clear that even Josiah's reformation would not save Judah (23:26-27) but what follows is a dismal catalogue of failed and downright bad kings who did evil in the eyes of Yahweh. The crown is tarnished and the life of the nation corrupt. Two of them, Jehoahaz (23:31-35) and Jehoiachin (24:8-17), each reigned for a mere three months but in that brief period showed their worthlessness and idolatry, pathetically copying the evil of their ancestors. The other two, Jehoiakim and Zedekiah, reigned for eleven years each and invite further comment.

Jehoiakim was a nasty piece of work. Jeremiah speaks of his extravagant lifestyle, building a palace without paying

the workers (Jer. 22:13-14) and like Manasseh shedding
innocent blood and oppressing people (Jer. 22:17); there
is further evidence of this in Jeremiah 26:16-23. Unlike
Josiah who trembled at God's Word, Jehoiakim cuts off
and burns the scroll of Jeremiah's prophecies.

Two particular points are made here. The first is that
the Lord sent enemy raiders against Jehoiakim (24:2). The
Lord of history was judging as He punished this wicked
king. This fulfilled the words of the prophets whom
Jehoiakim despised and tried to silence (24:3). The point
of 24:4 is probably not only to underline the wickedness of
Manasseh but to show that it lived again in Jehoiakim.

The other interesting observation is 24:7. On the face of
it this is simply historical information about the growing
power of Babylon and the weakness of Egypt. But this was
the territory promised to Abraham (Gen. 15:18-20), the
territory conquered by David (2 Sam. 8:1-14) and ruled over
by Solomon (1 Kings 4:21). That land was now trampled by
foreign armies and its days were numbered.

Zedekiah was not so much wicked as weak;
a weathercock apparently incapable of making up his mind
on anything. Again Jeremiah has more to say about him
(see e.g. Jer. 37-39). He seems to have been completely
under the control of his advisers and his ill-considered
rebellion against Nebuchadnezzar led to the final tragedy.

The Fall of Jerusalem (25:1-21)
The account here is virtually identical to Jeremiah 52 and
this is one of the reasons it is hypothesised by some that
Jeremiah was the author of Kings, although both could have
been drawing from a common source. The chapter first of
all talks of the dreadful fate of the last king to sit on David's

throne. The man who played for safety suffers far worse than he would have done if he had heeded the words of Jeremiah. He showed himself a false shepherd, abandoning the flock to the wolf then running away himself. Such was the end of this feckless and vacillating individual.

God's city and temple were destroyed; the flames would spread rapidly and the city of the Great King was reduced to rubble. The furniture of the temple (vv. 13-17), so lovingly assembled back in 1 Kings 6 and 7, is now dismantled and destined for the temple of Marduk. Yet we are to read of these again. In Daniel 5:3 they are desecrated at Belshazzar's drunken party and we know the end of that story. In Ezra 1:7-11, they are returned to Jerusalem for use in the rebuilt temple. But now all that is in the future.

The overall impression is of an undoing of the Exodus; that is how serious it is. This is not simply a mass deportation dreadful as that is but an apparent undoing of every aspect of Israel's faith. The heart of the Exodus story (see Exod. 12:12) is that Yahweh had defeated the gods of Egypt. Does this now mean that Yahweh is weaker than Marduk, head of the Babylonian gods? What of the promise to David of a continuing house and kingdom (2 Sam. 7:16)? They were back in the land that Abraham had left; to use C. S. Lewis' term this was a 'pilgrims' regress'. How could Yahweh not only have allowed this to happen but brought it about?

Mayhem and muddle (25:22-26)
But before the sorry tale ends there is yet another episode showing that nothing had been learned. Again this is a brief mention of a story told more fully in Jeremiah; this time in Chapter 40:7–41:9. Nebuchadnezzar appoints Gedaliah as governor to care for the few left in the land. Gedaliah's

father Ahikam was one of the delegation Josiah sent to Huldah (22:14) and also intervened to save Jeremiah's life (Jer. 26:24). This was clearly an attempt to restore something resembling normality but it was not to be.

We are not told why Ishmael and his assassins acted as they did. Perhaps since he was 'of royal blood' (v. 25) this was a futile attempt to restore the Davidic monarchy. But in the Jeremiah passage Ishmael is shown to be a total disgrace; treacherous and a betrayer of hospitality. The result is that many of the people flee to a voluntary exile in Egypt, against Jeremiah's warnings (see Jer. 42–43). The curtain has fallen.

Long live the king (25:27-30)
Probably the best way to understand these verses is not as an irrelevant postscript as some have argued but as the beginning of the fulfilment of Yahweh's promise to David in 2 Samuel 7:14-15. There stern punishment is promised for disobedience, now unfolding at the end of Kings, yet covenant love will continue and David's kingdom will endure.

Nebuchadnezzar's son, Evil Merodach, releases Jehoiachin from prison and elevates him to the highest status above the other vassal kings in Babylon. True, he is still a subject, but the author calls him 'king of Judah' (v. 27). Neither Judah's apostasy nor Babylonian imperialism can overturn the everlasting covenant. Zion is down but not out.

There is still a long way to go but when we come to Matthew 1:12-16 we find that the Davidic line has not died out and that the bleak story in 2 Kings 25 is a curtain but not the final curtain. And that hope is destined for even greater fulfilment. 'The Lord God will give him the throne of his father David, and he will reign over the house of Jacob for ever; his kingdom will never end' (Luke 1:32-33).

From text to message

Getting the message clear: the theme
Judgment is inevitable because of persistent disobedience and rejecting the words of the prophets. There is a note of hope but there is no cheap grace.

Getting the message clear: the aim
To show the seriousness of judgment and how God uses unbelievers to punish His own people if they reject Him. Yet the fact that God is Lord of history gives hope.

A way in
We often look at history including our own times and wonder why God's cause seems so weak and indeed for long periods of time and over large parts of the world seems to disappear completely. One reason for this, which we need to reflect on more than we do, is because of disobedience and complacency. Yet there is always a remnant and one day the earth will be filled with the glory of God.

Ideas for application
+ The total futility of idolatry and evil is powerfully emphasised and this is well brought out by Davis.[1] It is boring and meant to be. When we lose sight of the

---

1. 'Nothing bracing or refreshing here, just the same old stuff. None of the trembling faith of a Hezekiah or enthusiastic obedience of a Josiah that gives spice and flavour and drama to kingdom life', pp. 328-9.

Gospel there is nothing left but our own interests and abilities and why should anyone listen? The Gospel is inexhaustible and there are always new vistas to explore but unbelief carries on in its own monotonous way which admits of no development and leads nowhere.

+ We need a robust theology of history such as Habakkuk commenting on this era has, 'I am raising up the Babylonians' (Hab. 1:6). Similarly, here the Lord sends raiders to destroy Judah (24:2). That is grim but it also contains hope. The fall of Judah is no accident of history and the Lord who brings down to dust can restore to life.

+ The Word of God is powerful and active in bringing about these events (24:2-3). That Word whether in judgment or blessing will not return unfulfilled. (Isa. 55:11)

+ There is hope for David's line not because of the credibility of the last occupants of his throne but because of God's eternal purposes. 'The Lion of the tribe of Judah, the Root of David, has triumphed' (Rev. 5:5).

Suggestions for preaching

It is probably better to treat the material in one sermon although, as always, preachers will have to make up their own minds and some might wish to preach one sermon on 23:30-24:20 and focus on the different kinds of evil and their effect.

I would suggest as an outline on the whole section the following perhaps using the title given to this chapter.

Introduction
A condensed look at 23:30-24:20 focussing on the futility of evil whether in three-month or eleven-year reigns and the same dismal result whether there is weakness or wickedness.

The main body of the sermon would then have four sections:

David's king is dead (25:1-7) – Shepherd failed and sheep abandoned

God's city and temple destroyed (25:8-17) – is Yahweh weaker than Marduk?

God's people deported and dispersed (25:18-26) – bleak words of 21b – Babylon and Egypt swallows them up

Long live the king (25:27-30) – Line of David preserved and given honourable position

Suggestions for teaching

Questions to help understand the passage

1. How do we know from 23:32 that Judah is doomed?

2. What evidence is there that Jehoaikim was oppressive? See 23:35 and Jeremiah 22.

3. What is the significance of 24:7?

4. Why did Nebuchadnezzar deport the kind of people he did to Babylon? (24:14)

5. Why is Zedekiah compared to Jehoiakim? (24:19)

6. Why is there an emphasis on the furniture of the temple? (25:13-17)

7. What is the significance of the Gedaliah episode? (25:22-26)

8. Why is Jehoiachin called 'king of Judah'? (25:27)

Questions to help apply the passage

1. How do we know that Jehoahaz did evil even though he reigned for only three months (23:31)? Early days are often very significant in assessing character.

2. What do we learn from 24:2 about how God works in history? Can we think of contemporary examples?

3. 'The LORD was not willing to forgive' (24:4). Why?

4. Why is there a lot of emphasis on the temple? Read again 1 Kings 7 and 8 and reflect on how the temple symbolised God's presence among His people.

5. Why does the author include 25:27-30? What does this teach about both judgment and grace?

EPILOGUE

The book of Kings is part of the great story which was written both as example and warning for us (1 Cor. 10:11-12) and as such is far more than ancient history. Indeed the ultimate meaning of the Old Testament is that it is totally relevant to the last days when the Messiah has come. This does not mean we ignore the stories in their own right but that we see them as a vital part of and not simply a preparation for the Gospel. The Bible is one story, of one people of God, with one Saviour, one salvation, one song, one journey and one destination.

Two final observations can be made. The first is to emphasise the point made in the introduction that we need to take the book as a whole and not simply see it as a quarry for purple passages. Over and over again, these less attractive parts are a necessary background for the gripping and exciting parts. Would Elijah's ministry seem so powerful if it were not for the inept reigns of the likes of Nadab (1 Kings 15:25-32) and the evil of Omri (1 Kings 16:21-27) and especially Ahab? Would Hezekiah and Josiah be so magnificent without the contrast with Ahaz and Manasseh?

The second is that above all this is a story of grace, not least in the closing four verses. Judgment is real and just but grace is there and triumphs in the end unless it is rejected. This story is our story about sinners rescued from the judgment we deserve and made children of God. No one can read this book without being profoundly challenged and humbled, yet at the end the overwhelming feeling is of gratitude to Immanuel, the true King to whom the narrative so fully and faithfully points.

FURTHER READING

Kings is better served by commentaries in recent times than it often was in the past. Older commentaries tended to focus on the search for hypothetical sources and were marked by a rationalistic dislike of the supernatural. Such commentaries, while often helpful on matters of language, are virtually useless to the preacher. Recognise commentaries for what they are: resources to get us more deeply into the text and different kinds will give different kinds of help. A heavyweight commentary will give guidance on language and background and help us not to base sermons on mistranslations or inaccurate information.

Commentaries written by preachers will seem more immediately relevant but we need to be careful not to copy other people's sermons.

Three commentaries have been particularly helpful in different ways:

Dale Ralph Davis, *1 Kings, The Wisdom and the Folly* (Ross-shire, UK: Christian Focus, 2008); *2 Kings, The Power and the Fury* (Ross-shire, UK: Christian Focus, 2011). This is a sparkling commentary by a preacher who has also researched the background thoroughly.

Iain W. Provan, *1 and 2 Kings NIBC* (Massachusetts, USA: Hendrickson, 1995) – a concise running commentary which takes text seriously and is concerned with NT application.

Donald J. Wiseman, *1 and 2 Kings* (Leicester, UK: IVP Books, 1993) – this is especially helpful on historical matters but does not neglect theology.

Other commentaries which have been particularly helpful to me in writing this volume are:

John W. Olley, *The Message of Kings* (Nottingham, UK: IVP Books, 2011)

Lissa M. Wray Beal, *1 and 2 Kings* (Nottingham, UK: IVP Books, 2014)

Walter Brueggemann, *1 and 2 Kings* (Macon, Georgia: Smyth & Helwys, 2000) – this is often very perceptive on individual stories; less so on the flow of the narrative.

Those looking for a detailed engagement with the Hebrew text can find that in the two Word commentaries: Simon J. DeVries, *1 Kings, Vol 12* (Waco, Texas: Word Books, 1985) and Thomas R. Hobbs, *2 Kings, Vol 13* (Waco, Texas: Word Books, 1986). Both are useful on language and Hobbs very helpful on history; however, DeVries is unnecessarily sceptical.

Those looking for more on historical background (although Wiseman gives probably most that is needed) could consult Iain Provan, V. Phillips Long and Tremper Longman III, *A Biblical History of Israel* (Louisville, Kentucky: Westminster John Knox, 2003), a cogent defence of the historicity of the Old Testament.

PT Resources

RESOURCES FOR PREACHERS AND BIBLE TEACHERS

PT Resources, a ministry of The Proclamation Trust, provides a range of multimedia resources for preachers and Bible teachers.

Teach the Bible Series (Christian Focus & PT Resources)
The Teaching the Bible Series, published jointly with *Christian Focus Publications*, is written by preachers, for preachers, and is specifically geared to the purpose of God's Word – its proclamation as living truth. Books in the series aim to help the reader move beyond simply understanding a text to communicating and applying it.

Current titles include: *Teaching 1 Peter, Teaching 1 Timothy, Teaching Acts, Teaching Amos, Teaching Ephesians, Teaching Isaiah, Teaching John, Teaching Matthew, Teaching Numbers, Teaching Romans, Teaching Daniel, Teaching 1 and 2 Kings, Teaching the Christian Hope* and *Spirit of Truth*.

Forthcoming titles include: *Teaching James, Teaching Matthew, Teaching Mark* and *Teaching Leviticus*.

Get Preaching

Get Preaching is a series produced by the Proclamation Trust looking at a single issue integral to or associated with preaching. Whilst there are many comprehensive and even exhaustive books on preaching there are no titles that are solely focussed on a single area of the art, craft and science of preaching. That is where *Get Preaching* finds its niche. The idea behind *Get Preaching* is in two directions. *Get* preaching, as in understanding preaching, but also get *preaching* as in the hope that these books will equip, excite and encourage people to undertake the task of preaching.

The first titles in this seres are: *Get Preaching: Why Expository Preaching? Get Preaching: Preaching the Cross* & *Get Preaching: All-Age Services*

Practical Preacher series

PT Resources publish a number of books addressing practical issues for preachers. These include *The Priority of Preaching, Bible Delight, Hearing the Spirit* and *The Ministry Medical*. Forthcoming titles include a ministry checklist based on the book of 2 Timothy.

Online resources

We publish a large number of audio resources online, all of which are free to download. These are searchable through our website by speaker, date, topic and Bible book. The resources include:

- sermon series; examples of great preaching which not only demonstrate faithful principles but which will refresh and encourage the heart of the preacher.

- instructions; audio which helps the teacher or preacher understand, open up and teach individual books of the Bible by getting to grips with their central message and purpose.

- conference recordings; audio from all our conferences including the annual Evangelical Ministry Assembly. These talks discuss ministry and preaching issues.

An increasing number of resources are also available in video download form.

Equipped

Equipped to Preach the Word is a teaching series of 24 units, designed to provide a foundation for the work of expository Bible preaching and teaching. It comprises three modules, each of eight units, entitled *Equipped by the Lord* (module 1), *Equipped with the Skills* (module 2) and *Equipped with the Scriptures* (module 3).

The course can be accessed free at www.proctrust.org.uk/equipped.

Teaching the Bible Series

OLD TESTAMENT

TEACHING NUMBERS – ADRIAN REYNOLDS 978-1-78191-156-3

TEACHING JOSHUA – DOUG JOHNSON 978-1-5271-0335-1

TEACHING 1 KINGS – BOB FYALL 978-1-78191-605-6

TEACHING 2 KINGS – BOB FYALL 978-1-5271-0157-9

TEACHING EZRA – ADRIAN REYNOLDS 978-1-78191-752-7

TEACHING RUTH & ESTHER – CHRISTOPHER ASH 978-1-5271-0007-7

TEACHING PSALMS VOL. 1 – CHRISTOPHER ASH 978-1-5271-0004-6

TEACHING PSALMS VOL. 2 – CHRISTOPHER ASH 978-1-5271-0005-3

TEACHING ISAIAH – DAVID JACKMAN 978-1-84550-565-3

TEACHING DANIEL – ROBIN SYDSERFF, BOB FYALL 978-1-84550-457-1

TEACHING AMOS – BOB FYALL 978-1-84550-142-6

NEW TESTAMENT

TEACHING MATTHEW – DAVID JACKMAN, WILLIAM PHILIP
978-1-84550-480-9

TEACHING ACTS – DAVID COOK 978-1-84550-255-3

TEACHING ROMANS VOL. 1 – CHRISTOPHER ASH 978-1-84550-455-7

TEACHING ROMANS VOL. 2 – CHRISTOPHER ASH 978-1-84550-456-4

TEACHING EPHESIANS – SIMON AUSTEN 978-1-84550-684-1

TEACHING 1 & 2 THESSALONIANS – ANGUS MACLEAY 978-1-78191-325-3

TEACHING 1 TIMOTHY – ANGUS MACLEAY 978-1-84550-808-1

TEACHING 2 TIMOTHY – JONATHAN GRIFFITHS 978-1-78191-389-5

TEACHING 1 PETER – ANGUS MACLEAY 978-1-84550-347-5

TEACHING 1, 2, 3 JOHN – MERVYN ELOFF 978-1-78191-832-6

TOPICAL

BURNING HEARTS – JOSH MOODY 978-1-78191-403-8

BIBLE DELIGHT – CHRISTOPHER ASH 978-1-84550-360-4

HEARING THE SPIRIT – CHRISTOPHER ASH 978-1-84550-725-1

SPIRIT OF TRUTH – DAVID JACKMAN 978-1-84550-057-3

TEACHING THE CHRISTIAN HOPE – DAVID JACKMAN 978-1-85792-518-0

THE MINISTRY MEDICAL – JONATHAN GRIFFITHS 978-1-78191-232-4

THE PRIORITY OF PREACHING – CHRISTOPHER ASH 978-1-84550-464-9

About the Proclamation Trust

We exist to promote church-based expository Bible ministry and especially to equip and encourage Biblical expository preachers because we recognise the primary role of preaching in God's sovereign purposes in the world through the local church.

Biblical (the message)
We believe the Bible is God's written Word and that, by the work of the Holy Spirit, as it is faithfully preached God's voice is truly heard.

Expository (the method)
Central to the preacher's task is correctly handling the Bible, seeking to discern the mind of the Spirit in the passage being expounded through prayerful study of the text in the light of its context in the biblical book and the Bible as a whole. This divine message must then be preached in dependence on the Holy Spirit to the minds, hearts and wills of the contemporary hearers.

Preachers (the messengers)
The public proclamation of God's Word by suitably gifted leaders is fundamental to a ministry that honours God, builds the church and reaches the world. God uses weak jars of clay in this task who need encouragement to persevere in their biblical convictions, ministry of God's Word and godly walk with Christ.

We achieve this through:

- PT Cornhill: a one-year full-time or two-year part-time church based training course

- PT Conferences: offering practical encouragement for Bible preachers, teachers and ministers' wives

- PT Resources: including books, online resources, the PT blog (www.theproclaimer.org.uk) and podcasts

Christian Focus Publications

Our mission statement –

STAYING FAITHFUL

In dependence upon God we seek to impact the world through literature faithful to His infallible Word, the Bible. Our aim is to ensure that the Lord Jesus Christ is presented as the only hope to obtain forgiveness of sin, live a useful life and look forward to heaven with Him.

Our Books are published in four imprints:

CHRISTIAN
FOCUS

popular works including biographies, commentaries, basic doctrine and Christian living.

CHRISTIAN
HERITAGE

books representing some of the best material from the rich heritage of the church.

MENTOR

books written at a level suitable for Bible College and seminary students, pastors, and other serious readers. The imprint includes commentaries, doctrinal studies, examination of current issues and church history.

CF4•K

children's books for quality Bible teaching and for all age groups: Sunday school curriculum, puzzle and activity books; personal and family devotional titles, biographies and inspirational stories – Because you are never too young to know Jesus!

Christian Focus Publications Ltd,
Geanies House, Fearn, Ross-shire,
IV20 1TW, Scotland, United Kingdom.
www.christianfocus.com